Marcham P

The
Executive Secretary Guide to Building a Powerful Personal Brand

Anel Martin

Cover image by missimoinsane
http://missimoinsane.deviantart.com/

Thank you to my husband Raymond Martin, my coach and biggest supporter.

My mother Antoinette Blignaut, my role model and my first glimpse of what a special and authentic brand looks like in action.

My wonderful friend and global icon in the profession, Lucy Brazier.

The Gals: Susan Engelbrecht, Michele Thwaits, Cathy Harris and Teri Wells for the faith, support and guidance over the years. You light the way!

Marti Beukes, my friend, mentor and a world class assistant. You will never know how much you taught me over the years without even knowing it!

The Guinea Pigs: My Telkom peers and industry friends who helped me test my ideas and acted as a sounding board when I was in doubt.

All the delegates I have met all over the world, who have inspired me with their passion, their commitment and their questions!

Contents

1

Introduction

What is a brand?

There are many different definitions and understandings of the word and concept of brand. In this book I will <u>not</u> be focusing on the theoretical, "marketing textbook" explorations and definitions of the word.

These thoughts are my own and the ideas contained within are things I have either seen in action through observation or experienced in my own life. I have been blessed in my career to have met, interacted with and observed some of the best assistants in the world. What follows is what I have learnt.

In this book we will be delving into what it takes to create an authentic and powerful personal brand based on character, competencies and consistent behaviours in the real world. This book is not about "advertising" or "creating an image". What I will advocate in the book that follows is that you do the work consistently and build a reputation of value instead of faking it.

In essence, I believe your brand consists of the elements that make you unique and ultimately successful. It is the rare combination of traits and skills that combine to create **"YOU"**. It is the value and quality that people perceive in you, *be it real or in their minds*. Simply put, it is what people say and think of you when you leave the room.

You cannot fake an exceptional personal brand; there is no easy way to create it and no quick fixes for a damaged one. It will require hard work, discipline and an honest exploration of who you really are, what you want and what you stand for. It requires sincerity and constant course corrections over time to ensure that your brand remains consistent, on the right track and above all valuable and desirable.

The origin of the word brand comes from the Old Norse word "brandr" which means "to burn". Cattlemen used hot irons to burn their individual marks (brands) into their animals so that they could distinguish their own livestock when they go missing or are stolen. This system of creating a distinguishing mark, logo or brand came into popular use during industrialisation when sellers wanted to differentiate their products from similar ones to ensure that buyers would select their specific product and in that way increase their profits.

The origin of the word is so fitting, as it is my opinion that our brands too, should set us apart in the world. **They should be clear, singular and convey a strong message**. They should be recognisable and instil trust in others.

A potent, genuine brand is especially important in our roles as office professionals. In our roles we are expected to not only project an image of professionalism, discretion and competence but also produce on this "promise".

We tend to think of branding as a modern concept but in fact it is ancient. The first recorded brand was a herbal paste from India dating back to 1100 B.C.E. The focus on personal branding, however, is a more modern phenomenon. It has come into sharp focus with the advent of social media, which has given us the power to engage, learn from and share with people from around the world. We can now voice our opinions in a way that was limited to broadcasters only a few years ago. Social media has also made it easier to showcase our brands than ever before. We will look at this in more detail later on in the book.

I am excited to share my thoughts on brand building with you and I hope that you will enjoy this journey with me!

Who needs a brand and why?

In the modern world there are so many generic, knock-off or similar products that businesses and individuals need to focus on their unique selling points (USP)/special features, customer service and the end-to-end experience to get (and stay) ahead in the game.

As unemployment and retrenchments are soaring in many countries around the world there are more individuals competing for fewer positions and resources. This makes a powerful personal brand more important and valuable than ever before.

We all need to be distinct from others in the same group to give us that competitive edge! You want to be the candidate they remember from the interview, the person who is top of mind when a new internal position or opportunity becomes available. It is in these situations that we clearly see the value of a good brand.

Office professionals for many years have tried to blend in and be "behind the scenes" people. But in a more competitive world this has become an outdated notion. Every one of us needs to define and refine our own personal and professional brand to remain viable and relevant in the workplace.

Sadly, even if you don't see the value of a "brand" you already have one (good or bad) which you create daily with every interaction, conversation or piece of work delivered. What matters is that you create, manage and promote your own brand effectively to ensure that the performance appraisals, possible promotions and other opportunities go your way. Leaving your brand to chance is unwise. It should be something that you are aware of and that you consciously create.

In many companies the brand (which is an intangible asset) is often *as valuable as or more valuable than* the physical assets that the company owns; the same applies to our careers in any role we choose. It's not only what we do, but also what people believe about us that influence the value (material and otherwise) that they ascribe to us.

What does a successful personal brand look like?

In my opinion, there are two layers to a successful assistant brand. The first (or foundation) layer is the part that is expected as part of the role: the "Assistant Promise" if you will.

These are elements that are expected from exceptional assistants by virtue of the role itself and you will never create an extraordinary brand of your own as an office professional if these essential building blocks are not in place and solid.

These standard requirements for our chosen profession I like to refer to as the "Assistant DNA". This is by no means an exhaustive inventory but can be used as a checklist.

In my experience, all the really incredible assistants that I have met all over the world had the following in common (*I am sure you can think of more*):

    I Passion and commitment

   II Attention to detail and incredible logistical skills

  III Pride in the product and their own performance

  IV Emotional intelligence and real care for others

   V Intelligence and common sense

  VI Practical ability to see tasks through to completion

 VII Ability to plan and proactively avoid problems

VIII Well-spoken, confident and assertive

  IX Well groomed

   X Discrete and trustworthy

  XI Competent and highly skilled

 XII Informed about their companies and the world at large

XIII Humble and service orientated

XIV Organised and disciplined

 XV Positive

XVI Able to work with little or no supervision

XVII Able to work under pressure and be extremely resilient

These are some of the standard features. So how did you score on my list? Are you in agreement? Not all of us can display all these attributes 100% of the time but if we want to be in the elite group of assistants globally this is what we need to aspire to and work towards daily.

In addition to these standard features we all need to identify and develop our own special features. These unique attributes or skills are what set us apart from the pack. We need to analyse what it is that makes us distinctive and put it to work in our careers. Stick with me and we will explore how you can identify and utilise your unique features later on in this book.

What are the values/advantages of a successful brand?

A successful personal brand comes with many advantages. My own personal brand has enhanced my career in many ways and I can earnestly say that it is worth the work. A solid brand, built with integrity, will enhance your standing in your organisation and among your peers and within your profession. It will enable you to have a better understanding of who you are and what you stand for which then becomes like an internal guidance system, which will keep you on track.

It will also come with financial and opportunity-based advantages. A respected brand tends to be in higher demand. You will be more secure during times of flux in your organisation such as retrenchments or restructuring. Why? Well, you have defined your areas of speciality, you add value to your manager and team and you put your talents to work for the good of the company so you are less likely to be adversely affected by these kinds of changes.

In the worst case scenario when you do need to apply for another position you will have greater confidence when you need to be interviewed, you will have a strong network outside of your organisation who can assist you with identifying possible positions (or recommend you for suitable roles) and you will be aware of how your online presence could affect your prospects. A strong brand will also draw people and opportunities to you.

Amazing things happen when you understand what you can offer the world and when you start to seek opportunities to enhance the lives of those around you by offering the best that you have within.

A good brand and work ethic will ensure that you become successful in your role and that others view you and the profession with more respect.

Don't just take my word for it… *there are many assistants in the world today who are living proof!*

2

What is your current brand health?

How do we analyse our own brand health?

To create a stellar brand you need to first understand the current health of your brand. It will be the base that you build from and you need to take a long, hard and sincere look at yourself and your daily performance.

You will need to analyse your habits, routines, interactions and current competencies in a brutally honest way if you want to improve. It is always hard to have a realistic view of ourselves, so I would advise that you consult with a friend as well as a colleague that works closely with you and that you trust. There is a beautiful Irish proverb that says, "A friend's eye is a good mirror", so put these mirrors to use. Seek input and discuss what others see and experience about you. Sometimes these discussions will highlight and bring to the surface things that you never really thought about yourself. Often how we see ourselves is very critical and these discussions bring out a much more balanced and holistic view.

I would also highly recommend that you ask for input from your manager and team, and use this as constructive guidance on what you need to do to improve and shift your performance to the next level. This can be a painful process but nothing worthwhile in life is easy. This will require exceptional emotional intelligence and introspection on your part but it will be well worth it in the end. This process will be meaningless if you become defensive, sensitive or try to justify your position. Remember that you are <u>using</u> this feedback to develop and obtain better results.

It is also an ongoing process. A successful brand is not a one-off exercise. We have to maintain, refine and adjust it to remain relevant. What I am describing will require regular exercise – personally I try to review every six months but make additional course corrections as and when required.

Your performance appraisal is the perfect time to get input from your manager and team annually and it will have great value to you if you can incorporate their feedback during the year in preparation for the next session. If we do this "stock take" regularly we will not stagnate, we will improve year on year and start to innovate and keep ourselves up to date with trends and organisational changes. We will also be able to track our own development, which can be a very satisfying process.

Practical Brand Health Assessment Worksheet

Below is a checklist to assess your current brand health. Please use the checklist and indicate either **yes**, **no** or **sometimes** with regards to each question, and check your score at the end.

This checklist is personal and for your eyes ONLY. So I would ask you to be as honest as you possibly can to get the most realistic picture of the current state of affairs.

If you don't know how you rate on a specific question then get input from a trusted source.

This is not a scientific assessment, this should serve as a guide to you, it should help you look at brand building and eroding behaviours, and elicit questions and observations of your own about how you function in the working world and within your role.

Remember: No brand is perfect; the reason that you are reading this book is that you want to improve and enhance your current brand and this assessment is designed to give you a glimpse of where you need to start from.

Populate your answers in the table below or do the assessment online at http://www.anelmartin.co.za/brand-health-assessment.html

Let's begin…

Question	Yes	Sometimes	No	Your Score
1. Are you a punctual person?				
2. Are you always neat and groomed in your appearance?				
3. Would you classify your office environment as neat and professional?				
4. Would you rate yourself as friendly and courteous?				
5. Would you say that you get on well with other people the majority of the time?				

Question	Yes	Sometimes	No	Your Score
6. Do your personality and relationships help you to get things done with more ease?				
7. Can you produce consistently good work under pressure?				
8. Do you often miss deadlines?				
9. Are you assigned tasks that are not necessarily part of your current role?				
10. Does your manager ask you for your opinion on important decisions or changes that they need to make?				
11. Do people approach you for advice, be it personal or work related?				
12. Would you describe yourself as discreet?				
13. If your manager left the company would you have other options within the company and could you move to a new division with ease?				
14. Do you have outbursts or angry, loud confrontations or engage in office gossip or politics?				

Question	Yes	Sometimes	No	Your Score
15. Are you prone to sulking or giving people the silent treatment?				
16. Do you use your positional power inappropriately from time to time?				
17. Do you have a good relationship with the other assistants in your team and company?				
18. Are you giving some of your time to transfer your skills to others?				
19. Do you have a task list or organise the work that needs to be done daily?				
20. Are you absent from work more than you think you should be?				
21. Do you miss calls often, have a landline which goes unanswered or reply to emails very late?				
22. Are your submissions often returned for corrections?				
23. Are you someone who has a good eye for detail?				

Question	Yes	Sometimes	No	Your Score
24. Would you describe yourself as someone who communicates confidently and convincingly?				
25. Do you know what makes you special and do you put your talents to work				
26. Are you well versed in all the software packages that you are required to use during your working day?				
27. Would you describe yourself as having above average language ability?				
28. Do you have exceptional ability in working with statistics or numbers?				
29. Is your turnaround time on requests excellent and does the product that you produce always meet expectations?				
30. Are you an intelligent all-rounder who understands the business and the world that you work in?				
TOTAL				

Please remember that this is not a competition and it is not about the final scores. This is about finding a baseline and working on measures to improve the current state of your brand. Brand building is a daily exercise, it is not a project that you undertake once and it is finished.

Scoring:

Question	Yes	Sometimes	No
1	10	5	0
2	10	5	0
3	10	5	0
4	10	5	0
5	10	5	0
6	10	5	0
7	10	5	0
8	0	5	10
9	10	5	0
10	15	10	0
11	10	5	0
12	15	10	0
13	15	10	0
14	0	5	10
15	0	0	5

Question	Yes	Sometimes	No
16	0	0	5
17	10	5	0
18	10	5	0
19	10	5	0
20	0	5	10
21	0	5	10
22	0	5	10
23	10	5	0
24	10	5	0
25	15	10	0
26	10	5	0
27	10	5	0
28	10	5	0
29	10	5	0
30	10	5	0

MAX TOTAL 310

Score interpretation

Your Score is 310-260 (Good Health)

Your brand is healthy. You have good relationships with people and can harness your network to achieve results. You are valued and respected in your team and because of your outstanding work ethic, you are in demand both in your company and outside. You are skilled and competent. People respect you as an expert in your field and would describe you as a seasoned professional. Your brand is a valuable asset that needs to be maintained. The biggest pitfall is becoming complacent and thinking that you have nothing left to learn and no growth is required. You are well positioned to become a 'premium' brand. *No brand is ever perfect so I encourage you to continue enhancing and growing your brand. Learn new skills, meet new people, mentor someone with less experience and continue to do the right things, right!*

Your Score is 260-160 (Average Health)

Your brand is doing reasonably well. There is room for growth and improvement. The goal for you should be the transition from good to great! In a more competitive world we cannot afford to be average or "good enough". The upside is that if you apply the basics consistently the results will be very noticeable indeed! You have a good foundation to work from and the sky is the limit if you make the decision to take your brand to a whole new level. *Every day is a new day. It's time to look at your rituals and see how they are influencing your results.*

Your Score is 160-0 (Poor Health)

Okay, firstly reading this book and being honest with the questions listed is brave and the initial step to your spectacular brand recovery. So, things haven't been all that great thus far and you have some hard work to do. The good news is that there is nowhere to go but up, up and UP! The chapters that follow will give you guidance to get back on track and turn your brand into a world class one. There are no quick fixes and no one can do this for you. I would urge you to think about what you want for your future. If you want to be a successful assistant then the time is NOW! *This is the first step to re-establishing yourself and your career. Good luck on your journey and I hope that when you do this questionnaire in six months from now that you will see a massive improvement!*

3

Tools for brand building

Let's be friends: developing a healthy inner life

I am a big fan of Steven Covey's *7 Habits of Highly Effective People* and completely agree with his theory that the first step to lasting and meaningful change and public success is working on the inner self first. Your inner world, the conversations that you have with yourself and your views have such a massive impact on who you ultimately become and what level of success you are able to obtain.

The inner development that you do will create the groundwork for all that follows. The importance of this cannot be overstated. This may require months of hard work from your side but the results will be noticeable and more lasting than anything you try to manufacture artificially.

We need to work on ourselves, our habits, behaviours and our skills, as well as our internal dialogue, before anyone in the world will see the change in us.

We need to take control of our circumstances and acknowledge that we are not victims, no one is forcing us and we always have choices (*even when we think we don't*). We can change our obligations into opportunities by changing our frame of reference and starting to view our lives more positively. We are the lead character of this show we call our lives and we need to take ownership and move from managing our lives to creating them!

Yes, I hear some of you say, "There is a global recession," or, "I hate my job but I need it, I have responsibilities." And, yes, these statements may be true, but what I am asking you is, can you change your reality, how you feel, respond and perceive it and, most importantly, change the story that you tell yourself about it?

Once your focus shifts from "THEM" back to **"YOU"** amazing things will happen in your life. The simple act of taking control (letting go of the victim inside) and doing the best you can with what you have, suddenly releases new energy, which opens new and exciting doors. The change will be visible and it will influence how others perceive and treat you.

Next, what we think and say about ourselves (and to ourselves) is extraordinarily important and exceptionally powerful. In the words of Henry Ford, "If you think you can do a thing or think you can't do a thing, you're right." Most of us are our own most vocal and violent critics. What we need to cultivate first and foremost is a friendship with ourselves. We need to get to know ourselves as we would a new friend. We should be generous with our praise when it comes to our own achievements (even the small ones). We are in a role where we do a thousand things right every day, and which no-one acknowledges. So I urge you to acknowledge your own success. Learn to give yourself a round of applause every now and then. This will help you to need less external affirmation.

We also need to cultivate a level of patience with ourselves. No one is perfect and we should always strive to do well, but we should ease up on ourselves when we make a mistake. This is an area where most assistants struggle. Be kinder to yourself, give yourself a break when you need one. You are not supposed to be perfect all the time. As the old saying goes, "Show me a man who doesn't make mistakes and I will show you a man who makes nothing."

We need to believe in ourselves and have a bit more confidence in our own abilities, take up challenges positively when they present themselves and stand up for ourselves when it is called for. We need to actively cultivate confidence – taking it slowly and achieving small wins. Set yourself a small goal or try something new. When you reach this milestone or do the new task successfully you will feel your confidence swell until you are able to take on bigger challenges and opportunities.

It is like a muscle that you need to work and stretch to grow. You cannot get toned if you lie on your couch; the same is true for confidence. If you shy away from challenge all the time you will never, ever build confidence.

In my own life it has been the opportunities that I have found the most daunting that have given me the best returns and the most pleasure. I want to encourage you not to shy away from great things in your life because of fear. The mantra you should start repeating to yourself is, "I can and I will."

The role of an assistant exposes us to a great deal of stress (dealt with in detail later) by proximity to management, as well as the emotional demands placed on us by others at work and at home. We tend to be the person that everyone looks to when they need help or when there is a crisis. Most of the calls I receive daily start with the phrase, "Hi Anel, could you do me a favour...." Or, "Hi Anel, I need your help…" This is the norm for most assistants in the world, I think.

It is wonderful to be able to help others when they really need it, but many of us are being abused because we are too kind and like to help others. I would ask you to become more assertive if you are one of those assistants who are bombarded by these kinds of requests daily, making it hard to get through your own workload. It really says something amazing about you as a person that you want to help your team and other colleagues but this should never be done at the cost of your "day job", your health, your private time with your family or your sanity. You are not a bad person for saying no, and learning to do so is not only liberating but also sometimes critical to your well-being.

Many assistants tell me they feel guilty when they say no to colleagues. But your guilt is misplaced. What you should really be feeling guilty about is that these requests take time away from things you should be doing for your direct manager/s or your family. So feel guilty about that instead. Understanding that you cannot please everyone will help you decide who you will focus on, which in turn makes the act of saying no to someone (who is not on that list) much, much easier! These kinds of demands can drain you immensely so you need to be focused on keeping yourself emotionally well, happy, rested and healthy. It is a bit like the safety briefing on the plane… *You need to get your own oxygen mask on before you can help anyone else.*

If you are tired, burnt out, empty or ill you are not able to perform at your best, be it for your manager/s, team or family. This is generally a massively neglected sphere of the assistants' life: we look after everybody but we are bad at looking after ourselves and view any kind of self-care as selfish and a bit of a luxury that we cannot afford. I really need all of us (*including me*) to start making this a priority as this is where it can all go horribly wrong.

The most important things we can do for ourselves on a personal level to ensure that we are able to perform at our best and maintain a successful brand are:

- ✓ Ensure that we look after our physical well being

- ✓ Learn how to say no

- ✓ Stop beating ourselves up

- ✓ Get very clear on our own priorities and goals

- ✓ Define the roles we play in our lives and rate them according to importance

- ✓ Learn to reframe negative emotions and experiences

- ✓ Learn to manage stress and build resilience

- ✓ Create a lasting friendship with ourselves and be a little kinder to ourselves

- ✓ Find some quiet time in our hectic schedule

- ✓ Build confidence

- ✓ Let go of self-doubt and fear

Consistency

This is one of the most powerful tools that you have in your brand building arsenal. Being consistent with the quality of your work, emotions, appearance and in your relationships is absolutely essential. This is a magic formula for building trust.

People know that you will do what you say you will do. They know what to expect when they interact with you and they come to have faith in you because you treat them all the same. Our teams are a lot like children, in that they see how you treat them in relation to others.

Favouritism in teams is always a destructive force. It erodes your credibility and should be avoided. It is natural for us to like some people more than others but this should never become apparent to those around you.

We have all at some stage known (or perhaps been) the colleague who was happy one day and then sulked or gave others the quiet treatment the next. How did you feel when you had to engage with this person? Well, personally, not knowing what frame of mind they would be in each day would always make me a bit nervous and feel a tad intimidated about the next interaction.

The same applies when it comes to quality of work... Imagine the scenario:

You have a team member who is absolutely brilliant at what they do but is a bit lazy. This person needs to provide inputs and work to you regularly that you in turn need to compile for your manager. One submission is absolutely incredible and the next few are below par. What happens to your trust in this person? Do you agree that you would have preferred average submissions that were consistent as opposed to one report shooting the lights out and the next being such a disaster that it needs to be completely reworked? I think you get the point.

Producing an excellent product one day and letting the boss down the next, negates the previous good performance. Your manager should know that once a task has been assigned that you will deliver the same quality at the same speed. If you are consistent it makes the people around you feel secure and this sense of security is a very basic human need. It also frees your boss from having to expend more energy checking up on you or worrying about what you will or will not produce.

Integrity

In my opinion this is one of the most fundamental aspects of the assistant role and one of the most admired qualities that any human being can cultivate. We should function with a level of discretion and integrity that should never be questioned. We often work with sensitive information and situations. Showing a high level of honesty and maturity will always stand you in good stead.

We need to understand what our personal and company values are and ensure they guide our behaviour and decisions. You may find yourself in an environment that is in direct opposition to your own internal values and at some point you will be forced or expected to do things that you are not comfortable with. This is when you need to make a choice. Do you speak up? Do you go with the flow? Do you walk away? This is a choice that only you can make, but having a good understanding of your own value system will guide you.

If your integrity is being tested or you are working for a manager whose values are in direct opposition to your own you will definitely experience much more stress at work. This kind of situation is seldom sustainable.

I define integrity as being able to do what is right (especially when it is difficult) and living in your own truth. The definition may differ for you but it is important that you decide what it is to have and display integrity in your own life.

I am really committed to keeping my word. This to me personally is how I demonstrate integrity regularly. It is in fact one of the cornerstones of my own individual brand. A commitment to do something is not a decision I ever take lightly and once I commit, I intend to deliver. No excuses!

If I make a commitment I will do everything in my power to honour my obligation – sometimes at great cost to myself, but it is always worth it. Keeping your word makes you reliable, and reliability is rare. When and how you commit and what you actually deliver will speak volumes about your work ethic and will be immensely telling about your brand. Working and living with integrity is powerful and highly admired by those around you. Let's be honest, we all respect individuals who display integrity and ethics.

Values

For many of us it is hard to define values, although we have them. For the purpose of this book I would say that I define values as follows: *they are the principles and standards of our behaviour as well as our personal judgements of what is important in life.*

So where do our values come from?

Well, values are formed by our family, friends, our upbringing and our education. In fact our values are shaped by all our human interactions and mostly formed unconsciously. We instinctively know what is right (for us) and what is not. What we believe to be true and fair. What kind of behaviour is acceptable and what is not.

It is very important to note at this point that values are not shared by everyone and your own values may not hold true for another person. I urge each of you to respect the values of others.

What you need to establish and clearly define for yourself is what your own personal values are. Once you have quantified this it will help you as an internal guidance system. It will assist you to make better decisions, it will direct you towards or away from situations that are not in congruence with your lifestyle or principles.

- Here are some examples of values:

- Family and love

- Determination and achievement

- Competency, efficiency and excellence

- Individuality, creativity, flexibility and diversity

- Equality, respect and empathy

- Integrity, credibility, honesty

- Service and loyalty

- Adventure and fun

- Wisdom, intelligence and innovation

These examples are just to get the ball rolling. Take some to think about and define your values in words and preferably note them down in some way.

Why is this important? Well, let's think about it this way. If one of your core values is the importance of family and your current role keeps you away from them more than you would like, then this will be creating internal conflict that will create stress for you. If your manager works crazy hours he/she may not value family as much as you do. When you push back and try to reclaim your personal time (to spend it with family) your boss may respond negatively. This misalignment is bad for your brand and it may be time to regroup, have an honest discussion or move to a division or manager whose values are more aligned with your own.

Another example would be: if one of your values is honesty and you work for a manager who always expects you to tell white lies to keep them out of trouble, this could cause issues for you and make your working life uncomfortable. Being caught out in one of these white lies is going to be really bad for your brand (and the boss's).

Values underpin your brand in a meaningful way; it helps you to define yourself together with your skills and competencies. Self-exploration will create a brand that is true, well defined and textured.

Authenticity

Authenticity is just another big word for "being real". Nothing puts people off like a fake smile, only being nice to them when you want something or being friendly to them and then gossiping behind their backs.

You cannot manufacture real connections in the workplace; as with your personal life, real relationships take REAL work.

Authenticity only comes when you know who you are and what you are about. Embrace the fact that you are a little different from everyone else: it's what makes you special! I read a quote, which really gave me a personal light bulb moment, "They laughed at me because I was different; I laughed at them because they are all the same" – Kurt Cobain.

Strive to be the "real you" as much as possible. The results of this can be overwhelming. Communicate and say what you mean, but never in a rude or hurtful way. Be sincere in your interactions with people, when you say hello and ask how someone is... Don't do it out of routine or on auto-pilot, ask because you care and you want to know the answer.

Greet people, smile and give compliments (and, most importantly, mean them). Talk to the security, cafeteria and cleaning staff regularly. Engage in a meaningful way with someone at least once a day. Listen to the colleague who is going through a rough patch, remember the special days in people's lives, and acknowledge the achievements of others in a personal way.

The modern workplace has lost some of its humanity and assistants can (and should) be the hearts of the organisation. Authenticity is a powerful tool that will enable you to live a life you can be proud of and develop a stellar career and incredible relationships.

Emotional intelligence or EQ

What is emotional intelligence? EI or EQ refers to the ability to perceive, control and evaluate emotions. Emotional intelligence gives insight into your own emotions and those of the people around you. Imagine a world where you were unable to discern if someone was sad or angry!

Without emotional intelligence we are unable to create healthy and sustainable relationships. Some very wealthy "successful" people in the business world today have very high IQ but exceptionally poor EQ. They are powerful and to all outward appearances they are successful, but they have unhappy staff and unhappy marriages. They may get results but have teams with poor morale, high stress and ongoing churn. It can be exceptionally challenging to work in an environment like this and sadly I know that many of you who are reading this right now will be experiencing it.

Developing your own EQ will ensure that you are able to deal with this kind of situation and support others who are in the midst of it with you.

Personal assistants are expected to have superb EQ as we deal with many different stakeholders, sometimes under immense pressure. A great assistant can diffuse any situation, maintain their composure when the customer is shouting and put on a big smile (even if they're not really in the zone on a particular day). When emotional intelligence is low, your brand really suffers. People who have low EQ cannot control their emotions. These are the individuals who have loud screaming matches, need to be the big dog and can't keep their egos in check, burst into tears in public spaces at the drop of a hat or give you the silent treatment and get passive aggressive (not all the incarnations of low EQ but some very familiar ones).

Emotional intelligence at its core has four basic elements:

1. Self-awareness

Self-awareness is the ability to look at and analyse your feelings and emotions. As the ancient Greeks said, "Know thyself". Introspection is a great tool. If you understand your triggers and responses you have more control over your emotions and you can relate better to others.

Awareness creates power and choice

2. Self-management

Self-management is the ability to control your emotions, manage your stress and be able to regulate and modulate your responses to others. Use the gap between stimulus and response to enhance your brand.

3. Social awareness

This is the ability to understand people and situations. It is the ability to put yourself into someone else's position, see their point of view and acknowledge that they too have opinions and emotions. Just because their life experience and their views differ from yours doesn't automatically make them wrong. This is also the ability to "read" the emotional undercurrent in a meeting, and gain clues about the emotions of others from their communication, be it verbal or non-verbal. Social awareness is also being able to tune in to others, being able to sense their joy or pain.

4. Relationships

This is how we relate to others; at its core are the essential skills of empathy and being able to build rapport. Empathy is being able to imagine how someone feels. People with good EQ tend to have strong relationships with others and large networks. People will describe them as caring and easy to talk to. Being able to build rapport is getting on the same wavelength with someone and making an emotional connection. Personal assistants (generally) are really exceptional at both empathy and building rapport, which is why they are in these positions in the first place. The really magical assistants I know are the ones who take relationship building and networking to a whole new level – which can be a great asset to being effective in this role.

So maybe you feel that your emotional intelligence needs work? Do not despair. Emotional intelligence can be developed and strengthened; it also gets easier as you mature with age. I would seriously recommend that you identify someone who you feel has great EQ and model your behaviour and responses on theirs until you feel an improvement in your own EQ. This is an exceptionally good way to learn better behaviours and responses.

I have a friend who I observe and model when it comes to developing my own EQ. Often, when she is not around I ask myself what Susan would do in this specific situation or how she would respond. This is really helpful to me and it could be to you too!

There are five ways to boost your emotional intelligence:

✓ *Learn how to identify, manage and reduce stress in the moment and in a variety of settings.* Stress automatically reduces your EQ; it has been scientifically proven that stress shuts down parts of the brain temporarily. The heightened adrenaline and cortisol activates a flight or fight response and often we will fight in these situations. Create stress management strategies that work for you. If you need to take time out, then do so.

✓ *Recognize your emotions and keep them from getting the better of you.* If you understand your feelings (and the fact that they are generated internally) you are better able to manage your responses and your relationships. No one can give you a feeling or trigger your emotions without your consent. You are responding to input and you have a choice of how to respond.

✓ *Connect with others by using all forms of communication.* Use your communication skills to connect with people. Non-verbal communication is a much, much more effective way to get a sincere and authentic message across. Use all the tools at your disposal and take the time to really listen with empathy to others.

✓ *Use humour and stay engaged when faced with challenging situations.* Sometimes a stressful or difficult situation can be diffused by a little bit of humour. Don't take yourself or your point of view too seriously.

✓ *Resolve conflicts positively and with confidence.* Don't leave conflicts unresolved. Approach the other person with an open mind and put the disagreement to rest. Analyse what you did to contribute to the argument and take responsibility.

And always remember that a core element to creating better emotional intelligence is taking responsibility. You are **RESPONSE – ABLE**. You can choose better responses to stress and those around you and your brand will be better for it!

Special features

An essential and often overlooked part of our development is finding our unique skills or special features. What makes you different? What are your talents and how can you use them to enhance your brand and career?

Sadly most of us (and most of our human resource teams) focus on our development areas. I want to pose a question: Are exceptional careers built on compensating for what you are not good at or finding your special skill and making a success in your career by putting this special power/talent to work?

I fully agree that we need to be aware of what we are not good at and ensure that we negate any negative impact from this. But we should spend more time and resources getting better at the things we excel at.

It is basic human nature. If I ask you now to name three things you are not good at, you will be able to list ten or more instantly. Yet if I ask you what you are exceptionally good at, most of you won't be able to tell me. This is absolutely normal, but still a little sad.

This is possibly the most important question that you need to pose to yourself as this is your differentiator –the element that will make you marketable and remarkable. I want to assure all of you that you **do** have something special, you just need to take the time to find it. To you your special talent may seem insignificant or you may not be able to see it yourself. Again, a discussion with a close friend, partner or colleague could help you shed some light. I found the book *Now Discover Your Strengths* by Marcus Buckingham and Donald O. Clifton exceptionally helpful in identifying my own unique selling points and would highly recommend this to anyone who is having difficulty with this process. We will explore this in a more practical way later in this book.

Resilience

My definition of resilience is the ability to absorb and process stress. Being able to release it in a healthy way and reset properly. Resilience is an essential skill that we all need to develop. It's not that you don't feel stress or that it is easier for you to cope with than it is for others. It is your ability to handle it and get over it.

I love the metaphor of the branch that bends (stress) and then bounces back (resilience). Without resilience you will snap. Resilience also makes you more able to deal with changes in your life and be more adaptable and flexible.

In the words of Charles Darwin, "It is not the strongest of the species that survives, nor the most intelligent that survives. It is the one that is most adaptable to change."

So why is resilience important to brand? Well, if you can't reset properly it will affect your day-to-day performance, which in turn will affect your brand negatively. Stress keeps being mentioned because it really is one of the main factors that affect how we function, how we interact with people and our own morale. We also live in a world that is constantly changing, if we cannot adapt and survive we will not be successful and we will definitely not be healthy or happy.

If you are experiencing chronic stress you may lose the will to do the job properly, and become so overwhelmed that you choose to withdraw completely. Your interactions with others and your actual personality may change. Naturally this will impact on your performance and even your appearance. None of which is doing your brand any favours.

So how do we build resilience?

- ✓ Think about what is stressing you; will it matter in five years (getting perspective on the problem)?

- ✓ Get enough sleep

- ✓ Find healthy ways to decompress

- ✓ Get things out of your system by whatever way works for you

- ✓ Do something nice for another person

- ✓ Get some distance from the problem or do something to take your mind off it completely

- ✓ Surround yourself with positive, supportive people

✓ Remember that this too shall pass (no bad situation lasts forever)

✓ As cheesy as it sounds, remember that each day is an opportunity to start afresh

✓ Have a good laugh!

External world

In this part of the book we explore your outer world. How are you engaging with your stakeholders? What activities build or break down your brand when you engage with them and you live your daily life? Our inner and outer world interplay and you may see areas that overlap.

Not a single one of us is an island. We rely on people to get things done; in our role specifically we have a great deal of contact with other individuals. We don't always realise how we interact with others and what they really see.

Often the things that have the greatest negative impact on our brands are the smallest. Sometimes it is as simple as not greeting people, having a phone that rings which is not answered, not answering the phone in a professional way, responding late to an email or being abrupt with someone.

It's the little things that erode our brand daily. Luckily, they are also very easy to fix once you are aware of how important they are. Assistants are expected to be able to get on well with others. I keep saying this but think about it. The IT guy or the accountant in the office two doors down may not be expected to have people skills. When one of them is abrupt or rude they get a free pass as it is expected. Not so for us!

People skills are not a "nice to have" in our role, they are essential. They are central to how effectively you will function in this role and how successful you will ultimately be. The personal assistant role is designed for people who are able to interact with all kinds of people (irrespective of rank or income level) with kindness and respect.

Assistants are generally very effective in building relationships and genuinely care about others and offer their service to make the lives of other people easier and better. Office professionals generally display high emotional intelligence and are fantastic communicators. All these qualities make it easy for them to excel. Assistants are not necessarily extroverts; in fact some of the best and most powerful assistants in the world are introverts. In this book I am not advocating that all the assistants all over the world should suddenly become extroverts. Being introverted has many advantages in this role and building a successful brand is no easier if you are introverted or extroverted.

I am not asking you to broadcast your achievements or your brand to the world. I am asking you to live it sincerely. How we touch the world and how it touches us has a profound impact on our brand. In the segments below I will explain.

Behaviour

There are some basic behaviours that we all need to work on – not only to have successful brands but to be excellent in our roles as assistants.

Assertiveness – not to be confused with arrogance or aggression. This is the ability to be bold and decisive when you need to be. Learning how to say no with confidence and finding your own voice.

Friendliness, being able to engage. Being polite and having good manners. Speaking to people in a respectful way and touching them with your kindness.

Punctuality. A tardy assistant is always the one with the worst brand in the office. Always looked upon as lazy and a bit of a diva who swans in when it suits her/him.

Preparation is a habit and a behaviour. As office professionals we need to prepare for the day, week or month ahead. We need to ensure the equipment and venues are set up for meetings. Preparation is the key to efficiency and optimising your working life. Preparation is the key to making things look easy (something personal assistants are very good at). The old saying goes, "If you fail to plan, you plan to fail." Being prepared makes you look like you have control over the situation and it's fabulous for your brand.

Presence or charisma is often viewed as something that executives should have or something that you are born with. We all know that one person, when they speak everyone listens (even when they don't have anything profound to say). We also have that one colleague who is an absolute genius but cannot seem to hold people's attention or get his/her message across with impact. Well I am here to tell you that you can practise and learn presence! There are some simple hacks that you can employ to boost your own charisma or X factor.

Observation is a key tool in this process. Find someone in your office who has that special something. Take note of how they speak, move and interact. How do people respond to them? What can you try out?

Here are some basic tips to get you started:

- First, be real.

- Listen attentively and focus on the person you are talking to. Ensure you stay in the moment and make them feel important.

- Show your vulnerability when appropriate, coming across as human helps us connect with others who resonate with us when we share our shortcomings or problems.

- Be aware of what your voice is doing and how your body language is being perceived.

- Speak up confidently and assert yourself when you have the platform.

- If you don't like your voice try and get a coach and work on it if you can. This is central to how your level of charisma is received. A small squeaky voice will never be perceived as powerful. Good news is, it can be worked on and enhanced!

Having and displaying a positive attitude is not always easy. The real issue is that a positive attitude makes you nicer to deal with, makes you less stressed and depressed and actually gets you better results as you are focused on solutions, not blame or playing the victim. Let's face it, everyone prefers someone who is positive and who lifts them up just by being around, to someone who complains and worries all the time. This is exceptionally hard for us to do 24/7 but the results of being just a bit more positive about your situation will drastically improve your circumstances.

Dressing the part – any of you who know me personally will know that I am the very last person who should give fashion advice. But I do want to say to you that you need to dress appropriately for your role, your office and company. I am not advocating that you spend a fortune on your wardrobe. What I am saying is that you need to ensure that you are groomed, neat in appearance and dressed formally enough for your specific circumstances. Unfortunately the world really does judge a book by its cover, so make sure that yours looks good!

Assistants as leaders

Few office professionals realise that they are already leaders in their organisations. Stepping into this role and becoming a fully fledged part of your management team is brilliant for your brand and your career.

We already manage others on behalf of our bosses and need to do so in a spirit of co-operation, not by using any kind of positional power. We need to get results without breaking down relationships. We need to use our powers of persuasion and our ability to get people to share our vision and get on-board with our ideas or what needs to be accomplished through our personalities and communication skills.

Assistants are also important players when it comes to team morale. The team takes cues from you, they assume that you have more information than they do about upcoming changes or what is happening behind the scenes in the organisation (*which is absolutely true in most cases*) so they watch how you respond. They follow your example. If you are negative, they will be too, so be aware that you are setting the tone more than you know.

Enthusiasm is your greatest tool. Having a clear plan, being able to communicate it effectively and being really excited about what you have to do is contagious. People respond to that in amazing ways.

Leadership expert John C. Maxwell says, "Leadership is influence". I couldn't agree more. Personal assistants have so much more influence than they realise. So what is influence? It is defined as, "The power to change or affect someone or something: the power to cause changes without directly forcing them to happen."

In the words of Kenneth Blanchard, author of *The One Minute Manager*, "The key to successful leadership today is influence, not authority." So if the leadership experts are saying it, then it must be true. If you look at your role I am sure you will see how much influence you have and how you are actually leading through this ability.

Maybe you don't see yourself as a leader or you feel you need to develop leadership skills. Well you have a front row seat at the game. You see high powered executives all day long; you see what they do and what they say, how they engage with people and how they use their authority and their influence, how they collaborate, and who the align themselves with. You see the games and the politics…

Some executives teach us what we should emulate and others show us the pitfalls of doing it the wrong way. *In either case you learn*. In fact, I have learnt more from the horrible bosses than the good ones (if I am honest).Ensure that you make use of this free management training. Pay attention to how they speak, write and behave. You can really learn a great deal from simple daily interactions.

Real leadership is leading yourself. There is a beautiful Latin saying, "Vincit qui se vincit", which means "she (or he) conquers who conquers herself (himself)". Being able to manage yourself and your life is a huge accomplishment in itself and will set you up for success in every sphere of your life. You will never be able to manage anyone else if you cannot achieve this. Once we overcome our own bad habits and flaws we can start to live a disciplined life, one in which we reach our goals through daily action towards them. This is the simple act of doing what nobody else is willing to do to get the results you want at the end.

This is perhaps studying part time (which is a challenge when you are in this role), which means that you need to commit time to learning. This means that you may be missing out on dinners and weekends to get the job done, which takes discipline. It's not fun while you are doing it but you are giving up on the immediate pleasure to get a bigger pay-off later on. And so it is with many things in our life. Sometimes we need to sacrifice what we want now for what we want <u>more</u>!

Another very profound lesson I was taught early on in my working life was to never ask anyone to do something that you are not willing to do. When you work and live from this frame of reference you immediately treat people with respect and dignity. You look at a task that is not pleasant and ask yourself if you would be willing to do it before you ask someone else to. You don't treat people like they are beneath you, only asking them to do the rubbish jobs you feel too special to do!

As assistants in high powered offices we should be careful not to build empires or start behaving like we are more important than we really are (we all know an assistant or two like this and it's not flattering). If you indulge in this kind of behaviour you are relying on your boss's positional power and not your own leadership ability or relationships. This is a brand breaker of note. It implies weakness on your part and does not project the power that you think it does. Using someone else's name to get things done just means your own name is not good enough. There is a time and place to pull the "boss-card" when trying to get things done but this should never be your default option or the only play you have.

Another important thing to remember is that if you don't develop your own name and leadership ability, you will be stranded if you are redeployed or if the boss suddenly leaves. You will be out in the cold because you have alienated others (whether you realise it/intended it or not). You will often find that assistants who have abused the boss's name and positional power find themselves isolated. People will not assist them when they move to a lower level in the organisation because of their previous behaviour.

Leaders love diversity, they realise that diversity equals opportunity. Diverse workforces have varied backgrounds, skills and opinions. Embrace all that your team mates have to offer. Try to learn from those who are different to you, listen to their ideas and take on board new information and skills from them that you can put to use for your benefit and the benefit of all.

Respected leaders have a vision, they create a plan and they execute on the plan. Leaders get results. Real leaders (not bosses) lead from the front and are able to get things done. Leaders also show genuine appreciation and make others feel important – *as opposed to thinking they are important.* They are good to people and they are humble. Truly great leaders also realise that the key to staying in the game is continuous development and learning, they don't know it all!

Effective people management is highly dependent on your ability to understand people and what makes them tick. One size does not fit all and you will need to adjust your approach for each individual to get the best results. As assistants we need to embrace the ideas and practical real world activities that come with being leaders, even if we do not have titles. We are not assistants, we are business partners. Leadership through influence is the core element that will raise the profile of our profession and will have great brand-boosting side-effects for you personally. If we want to be taken seriously by the business world, then it's time to GET SERIOUS!

Competencies and continuous development

In the good old days, all an assistant needed to be able to do was type, make a great cup of tea, look fabulous in a pencil skirt, answer the telephone and avoid the attention of the office perv. Oh my, how the world has changed!

With organisations scaling down their headcounts, assistants have taken over numerous middle management functions like finance, HR, and project management (to name but a few). Office professionals now need to be on the cutting edge of new technology as they are often the early adopters in the organisation of new equipment, operating systems or software packages. Sadly, very few have received any training or development from their companies to fulfil these roles or acknowledgment for the extra work that these new functions entail.

The good news is that office professionals are very resourceful, incredibly intelligent and are able to create development opportunities for themselves. We are often asked to do things that we have no experience or training in and somehow we just get it done! Often we achieve these objectives by the magic power of Google or by phoning up someone who can assist or provide us with advice. We learn as we face new challenges and by doing this we expand our skill sets and experience exponentially each year, something that few other employees in other roles can emulate.

It is essential that YOU take your development seriously (*even if your company doesn't*). Being highly skilled will make you more marketable (and a great deal more valuable) and soon you will have the opportunity to move on from where you are not appreciated or respected to something much, much better, simply because you took the lead on your own learning and development. Make this your mission. Use the internet, read books, find a mentor/be a mentor, ask experts for help and just keep learning. Development does not have to cost money. Get creative and utilise everything and everyone that you have access to so that you can up your game. This is adding value to your brand, your CV and your life! Take ownership of the process; don't wait for others to do this for you, *because they won't!*

If you are in the lucky position that your company and, more importantly, your manager supports your development and is willing to invest in you with finances and time, then it is your obligation to make the most of these opportunities and give your company a phenomenal return on investment. Each time you attend a workshop or seminar make sure that you transfer skills to others who could not be there in person, apply what you have learnt actively and ensure that your management sees the value of making these kinds of opportunities accessible to more assistants. Show them that if they invest in you they will reap the rewards many times over!

Networking

It is important for us to create circles of people in our lives personally and professionally – people who can support and empower us and for whom we can do the same. Networking is not only meeting new people but creating mutually beneficial, long-term relationships. The key to success here is that the benefit is **mutual**. Networking should never be done with the idea that you can get something out of someone. This really puts people off. Don't use other people or try to exploit relationships for your sole benefit. Always try to find ways to interact with others in your network so that you can add value to them. If you do this the value will come back to you automatically and freely.

Networking can be done in person at events or even in your own office or online via business portals like LinkedIn or joining a professional association. Office professionals are creating very powerful communities online, which are easy to join and very supportive. Relationships are blossoming between people who have never met in real life across time zones and cultures. Social media has started uniting our profession on a global scale and this bodes well for the future. It has become a way to get advice, share knowledge and benchmark with your peers around the world.

How does networking enhance your brand you may ask? Well, it is a good way to position yourself within your industry; after all, **it is fantastic to be really good at what you do but a bit pointless if no one outside your office knows how good you are or that you even exist.** Having a strong network can create a steady supply of skills that you can harness when you need help and/or resources, it can provide you with collaboration opportunities and can even assist you to get your next job. It is not only about positioning and promoting your brand but also about connecting with others who have the same challenges and passions that you do.

Your manager may not understand why you need a business card or why you need to network, but don't let this stand in your way. Have your own business cards printed up and make sure that you join one of the numerous personal assistant/executive assistant social media platforms or local associations available to you. Better still join or create your own in-house forum for assistants. Personally I can attest to the power of these connections in my own career and life. They can create amazing opportunities and really meaningful professional relationships.

Networking is not only for the extroverts. If you are not comfortable with face-to-face social contact, then start small. Make it your goal to meet one new person at work in a month, talk to someone new while you wait in line for a coffee or in the lift. Join an online group where you do not need to be concerned about being socially awkward. *I promise, promise, promise that if you work at it, it will get easier and more enjoyable.* Introverts also have the great advantage that they tend to be much better listeners, often coming across as more authentic and sincere, so use that to your advantage.

Another essential tip is that if you get someone's business card or an invite request, respond promptly and keep in touch.

Relationship building

So how do we build relationships and how do we harness this to create more effective brands? Well, first, we find out who the influencers are in our company and profession. We try to establish connections with these individuals (networking) and then we go about trying to build and maintain real, lasting and beneficial relationships.

Gaining information and an understanding of the person is step one. Asking good questions and trying to find areas of common interest is a great way to start a relationship.

The simplest way to maintain good connections is by keeping in touch regularly, assisting when the other person needs help, being interesting and uplifting to be around and by being a caring person. These traits will keep people engaged. There is nothing worse for a relationship than only being interested in someone if they can do something for you. Make sure that if there is someone you rely on at work that you touch base with them regularly, not only when you are in trouble. Be interested in their lives and find out about them as human beings. Say thank you regularly and when you are around, go and say hello in person. Be supportive and willing to assist others in their time of need and I promise you that you will reap the benefits (not always from the same person but often in ways you would never have expected).

I have a very strict rule that when I deal with vendors/suppliers I only deal with one person if possible. The reason is simple. We establish a relationship, the person gets to understand my circumstances, they know how and when I need things to happen and, by building a meaningful relationship, they assist me when I am in need of help. A last-minute change to travel plans, a fast-track delivery of stationary for a workshop… You get the picture.

From my side, I say thank you and compliment them on a job well done, ensuring that their manager knows I have received good service. I will send flowers or a gift when someone has really gone beyond the call of duty. I try to meet them face to face and I treat them with respect.

Building healthy relationships with your manager and team is also good for your career in the long run. I am not talking about friendships (but this could happen too). I am referring to respectful business interactions, which take the stress and issues out of getting your job done. Work towards understanding what makes them tick. Sometimes just agree to disagree and always focus on the problem at hand and not the person. Be professional with your colleagues.

If you don't like a specific individual, make sure that you engage with them in a decent way. Don't let them drag you down to their level as this is not good for you or your brand. As mentioned before, assistants are expected to have good people skills and are held to a higher standard on this than other employees. Ongoing conflict (or even an under-current of conflict) can create a negative perception of you.

If you really don't like your manager or someone in the team, then start to treat them like customers (because that is ultimately who they are). You don't need to be over-friendly and you don't need to have an emotional connection but you do need to provide them with service and you owe it to yourself to act and behave like a professional. Again, move your focus from "THEM" back to "YOU". Being consistent, trustworthy and authentic will assist you in building solid relationships over time.

Focus on what you can add to the equation, not what you can get. Consider what is positive about the individual, not what is wrong, and I guarantee that your relationships will improve. Compliment others on what they have done right, and show appreciation when they have helped you.

Social media

Social media is very prolific in the modern world and it can enhance or completely destroy your brand and your career. Assistants are expected to be discreet, so make sure that your social media profiles don't create the impression that you are unsuitable for your position, irresponsible or that you are sharing information that you shouldn't.

Be mindful of what you post on social media. Make sure that you would be happy for your mother and the company CEO to see whatever you post online. Remember that this is in the public domain. Nothing done on social media should be considered "private". Keep controversial stuff OFFLINE!

If you post photographs make sure that they are appropriate and not something that will come back to haunt you at a later stage. No one wants to see their assistant dancing on the tables and partying it up on the weekends. Stay away from hot topics like politics and religion. Make sure that what you post is not negative in tone or something that will put people off or bring them down. Don't post sad obscure messages trying to elicit sympathy, don't post about every ailment you have. Don't constantly rant or criticise everything. There is enough negativity in the world!

On the up side social media is connecting us with one another professionally in a way never seen before. We have access to information and skilled individuals who for the most part are happy to engage with you and offer help. We also have global personalities and role models for the profession emerging and we also find out about events taking place in our vicinity.

Online platforms like LinkedIn are becoming online résumé sites and a great deal of headhunting is done from this forum. Recruiters and other interested parties routinely check out your social media profiles to see what you are all about, so it's critical that you keep it up to date, clean, appropriate and uplifting.

We can use social media to have a voice in the profession, contribute to the skills development of others by sharing what we know and providing advice. It can also be harnessed very successfully to promote your brand and upskill and encourage others.

Some simple tips for beginners:

- ✓ Keep your friends and relatives on Facebook (if possible).

✓ Business connections and professional interactions on LinkedIn (if possible).

✓ Always have a good professional profile photo for LinkedIn – this can really let you down if you don't have one or select an inappropriate one. I would recommend getting a good headshot done for this purpose.

✓ Make sure that you treat your LinkedIn profile like an online CV.

✓ Always keep it clean. Don't use bad language or offend others.

✓ Try and use social media to stay in touch with people that you meet in person at events.

✓ Make sure that you are projecting a truthful reflection of yourself on social media. Don't fake it!

✓ Make sure that when you post you have something worthwhile to share.

Curriculum Vitae/Résumé

It is very important for personal assistants to have beautiful and professional CVs. Our résumés are judged not only on content but, due to the nature of our role, are stringently reviewed for how they are actually compiled, from formatting to spelling and everything in between.

Your CV is your first impression. *Make sure that you don't blow it!* View this as a brochure of your services and your experiences. Think about what will make it stand apart from all the other résumés that will be received. Guarantee that you make an impact with this first contact and that you showcase your brand successfully, as this may be the only chance you get to land the job you really want. Mention your special features and how you apply them as this is something that makes you unique.

Confidently market who you are and what you do, but never lie or misrepresent yourself.

Stay away from any of the old clichés that people have on their résumés (like "I am a team player", "I am self-motivated"). Those things may be true but find another way to word it and ensure that you stick to the facts. You may only get one chance so make sure you get to the next stage of the recruitment process by "selling" yourself effectively. False/exaggerated humility or arrogance will definitely not help you here.

I always like to have a photograph on my CV so the selection panel can put a face to a name. But as with social media profile pictures make sure that it is appropriate and professional. Try to be concise and accurate. Ensure that you have references listed on your résumé that are contactable, ethical and will give you a good reference when called upon to do so. Adjust your CV if there are specific requirements from the recruiter's side like a maximum amount of pages, a specific section they want you to respond to or documents that you are required to submit. Your curriculum vitae should be a living document, routinely updated and maintained.

A poor CV will never get you shortlisted so if you feel insecure about your résumé ask someone to assist you. Also make sure that you have a CV on hand and up to date, even if you are in a permanent position that you are happy in. You never know when your circumstances may change or a great opportunity comes up. This should be part of your brand management activities. Just like you review your brand health, make sure that you are keeping your "brochure" up to date regularly.

Interviewing

Interviewing successfully is more art than science. It is about using the time you have to market yourself effectively to an audience that you usually don't know. Interviewing is a lot like auditioning for a stage show. The panel has something specific in their minds. They know what they are looking for and sometimes you are just not it. This should never put you off. The more experience you have doing interviews the better you will get at it. The interview starts when you have your first contact, be it by email or on the phone to invite you to come in and meet the panel.

Make the most of every single point of contact. Remember that you are being rated consciously or sub-consciously on how you respond to email or how you sound on the phone. Another basic is to be punctual and dress the part. It is pointless to be the best person for the job and then arrive late or look like you couldn't be bothered to dress appropriately.

Greet the panel with confidence and make good eye contact. I have been on many panels for assistants and I can tell you that many let themselves down by being too shy or soft spoken in the interview process. Remember the panel is looking at you and thinking about how you will interact with guests you have never met or strangers on the phone and also how you will deal with high pressure interactions.

When answering questions in a panel interview situation, make sure that you talk to each person, make eye contact and speak with confidence. Don't disrupt your own communication by making basic blunders like rambling, or umming and ahhing your message across.

You do need a certain amount of confidence. After all, if you don't believe you can handle the role, how do you expect the panel to believe you can? Someone once told me before an interview that you should think "give me the keys to your Ferrari, I am ready". This is just a little confidence trip, which has helped me, and it may help you too. Just always make sure your confidence doesn't look like arrogance. Talk confidently about your achievements, use examples of problems you encountered and how you solved them successfully and make a point of convincing the panel that you are competent and more than able to do the job.

When the panel asks you to tell them something about yourself, try to always work in something that could be relevant to the role. For example, if you do social media for a club or organisation, mention it in this part of the interview if you think that this may be of interest. Mention any hobbies that you may be able to apply to the role or part-time activities that may be relevant. The panel really doesn't want to hear about your pets or your sick grandmother.

Slow down and THINK. If you don't know how to answer a question ask if you can come back to it. Preparation is key. Before the interview, research as much as you can. Find out as much as you can about the company, the industry and the future boss. Get someone to ask you interview questions and prepare some of your own if you get the opportunity to ask the panel questions. If you ask some intelligent questions at this point you can completely blow away the panel and make an incredible impression.

Another tip from me to you is that you should never agree to something in an interview that you cannot live with. If they ask you if you enjoy figures and could handle the budgets and you don't like that kind of work, rather be honest. If the panel asks you if you are willing to travel but you have small children and it's going to be difficult rather don't agree to it and pass on the position. If you don't it will be a poor fit for them and, more importantly, it will also be a poor fit for you.

Instead, market what you can do, what you actually like and what will be sustainable for you as a person. Be true to yourself and your brand. You may lose out on that specific position but it's better than resigning a few months later because you hate it or worse still wasting years of your life in a role that is not suitable for you.

So, the interview has come and gone. Make sure you send a thank you email or make a call to the HR manager/recruiter to thank him/her for the opportunity to meet the panel. If you are unsuccessful contact them to find out if you can get feedback on the interview – where did you go wrong or how could you improve for your next interview? Most companies are happy to provide you with feedback and it is very useful for you. This feedback will be essential for you to improve your interviewing skills over time – if you can't ace an interview you cannot get hired!

Return on investment

So congratulations you got the job! You settle in, learn the ropes and then get to the business-as-usual stage. Sadly, this is where many an assistant lets themselves and the profession down.

When you get to work are you just killing time till you can go home? Are you on personal calls all day? Are you doing just enough to stay on the payroll but under the radar? Or are you providing an excellent service at a great price? Many assistants lose sight of the fact that they need to show a good return on investment to remain viable in a world where more people are competing for fewer positions and where assistants are trying to enhance how the role is viewed by the majority of business. Happily I can report that this is the minority, but they are still the minority who are giving the profession as a whole a bad name.

We should all think of ourselves as a business (because that is actually what we are).You are the CEO and service provider to your own company and you are your boss. Are you a good investment? How long will the company keep paying if it is not getting value for money? This is something to give some serious thought to.

As a small business owner we also need to become cognisant of the amount of time that we give away for free in unpaid overtime. Sure, there will be times when you are really needed for an emergency situation and I have no problem with that. My issue starts when this becomes habitual. A plumber won't come to your house and work for free, so why are we doing this? No business is run like that and it is not a sustainable business model.

We should strike a good balance between not putting in enough and respecting ourselves and our families enough to not put in too much. If you respect your product and your own time you can actually get a better price for it. In contrast when the boss is used to having you at their beck and call all hours of the day and night, plus weekends and holidays, and you never speak up, they won't offer you any compensation/time off or lose any sleep over it.

Ensuring that you keep up to date with trends, technology and other areas of development also ensures that you provide the best possible service. Another bad attribute of certain assistants is that they get to a point in their careers when they think they have been there and done that and that they don't need to learn or grow. When you ask them why they do a thing the way they do they will respond "it's how we have ALWAYS done it and it's the best way".

This is incredibly short sighted and this kind of mindset will make your skills redundant in a few years, put your head on the chopping block when your boss resigns or it's time for retrenchments and it will make it near impossible for you to get a new position. So, yes, by all means get comfortable, settle in and get to the business-as-usual stage but ensure that your skill set is always in the development phase.

Communication

Communication is how we touch our world. Needless to say, it is a critically important factor when it comes to your personal brand. How we speak, how we write and how we use our bodies and our faces impact how we are perceived. It influences how seriously people take us, how professional and competent they think we are and how we connect with people.

Communication is our greatest tool if used correctly. So, what do we have at our disposal?

Speaking is important; our voices, tone, pace and vocabulary create a picture of us. We need to speak with care and awareness; what we say and how we say it is incredibly important. You can have all the building blocks in place but if you speak negatively you will never get the required effect or impact from your verbal communication. So delivery and message are both incredibly important.

Listening is an absolutely essential part of communication, which is massively underrated. There are many programs designed to teach us to speak better but very few learning opportunities to teach us to listen. We live in a society that values talking but not listening. Listening is immensely important in the role of the personal assistant. If you do not listen well and ask good questions you will be ineffective in this role. Do not listen with the goal to respond or try to anticipate what the other person is trying to communicate. Suspend your own internal dialogue and try to listen carefully. If you can listen with concentration and empathy you will definitely enhance your communication more than by doing ANYTHING else. This really is the golden key to verbal communication and doing this well will make ALL the difference, not only in your professional life but also in your personal life!

When we write, we need to be aware of our grammar, tone and sentence structure. We need to structure our written communication in a way to get our message across as accurately and effectively as possible. We need to try and avoid creating any ambiguity in our written communication because we do not have the extra dimension of facial expression or tone to back up the real meaning. That is why you sometimes find that you write an innocent email and the person responds in an angry way. The receiver of your message has interpreted your message through their own set of filters, not necessarily in the way you intended. So be aware that written forms of communication have a limited scope and depth when it comes to sensitive issues.

Your body and face can also have a much bigger impact on what you say than you may realise. It is also massively effective in building rapport with others. When people speak to you they believe what your non-verbal communication is telling them if what you are verbalising does not match up with your body language. Body language can help or severely hinder communication so be aware of what your body and face are doing. People will believe what you do but not always what you say.

4

Brand breakers

Stress

Oh my goodness, by now you must be wondering if this book is actually about stress. No it isn't, but the impact of stress on your brand is severe and I will keep coming back to it. There is without a doubt nothing that can create brand havoc like stress. Stress is mentioned frequently in this book for just that reason. Stress can make us act out of character and can actually do lasting damage to our brands, our health, families and careers.

There are mountains of information available on stress and how to manage it effectively. Yet as a society, and as a profession, we are still suffering from acute, chronic and prolonged stress. In fact, the effects of excess negative stress are so severe, and are affecting so many people, that stress is now being widely referred to as the 'Black Death of the 21st Century'.

The word stress is derived from the Latin word 'stringere' which literally means "to draw tight". This is a wonderfully descriptive root word, which aptly captures how stress feels in the human body. Many of us can relate personally to this feeling of being pulled like an elastic band, fully extended and about to break.

Stress is normal, and as we all know, it comes in the good stress (eustress) and bad stress (distress) categories.

Good stress prevents boredom and enhances motivation. Many of us are at our most productive and creative when there is a looming deadline (definitely me!). Good stress enhances focus and concentration and gets us moving. For some of us there needs to be a specific amount of stress before we have the momentum to start working on something and we tend to produce our very best and most creative results under these conditions. We also tend to find more innovative solutions and our problem solving ability increases.

Bad stress is different! It's the feeling or perception that you do not have the resources to complete or achieve the task at hand. It creates imbalances in your life on all levels and can be crippling. It is associated with anxiety and even panic attacks in severe cases. You can feel so overwhelmed that you are not able to do anything at all.

As administrative assistants we are exposed to physical and emotional stress daily due to the nature of our profession. This prolonged exposure to stress can cause us to react to people and situations in ways that can be destructive. Ironically, our teams and bosses seem genuinely surprised when we say we are stressed. For some reason they think our jobs are easy and that we have nothing in our roles that can or should create any stress.

This is completely false and if you are in a situation where you are being treated in this way, just know that you are not alone. Many assistants globally are experiencing negative stress, which is exaggerated by their manager's, team's or partner's reaction to it.

When we experience stress we tend to act out. We are more abrupt with people, we may lose our cool and go nuclear or just simply meltdown and get emotional. Things that are induced by stress and trying circumstances are discussed in the early segments of this book.

Assistants are expected to get things right and be organised all the time – our margin for error is very small indeed. We are expected to anticipate the requirements of others and to be perfect and remember everything all the time. And yet we are human like everyone else. Sadly, we are the biggest perfectionists and place the highest demands on ourselves.

As the right hand person to a high-powered executive you are also exposed to their stress. A recent study by the University of Hawaii has found that stress is as contagious as the common cold. We therefore not only contend with our own stress (be it work or personal) but we are also exposed to our boss's stress due to the close working relationship that is unique to this specific role.

Another cause of distress is hyper-connectivity and poor life balance caused by technology and working for companies that have offices in different time zones. We are currently living in a society that never shuts down and we are being engulfed by waves of information that hit us on a daily basis in the form of never ending emails, reports and statistics.

Smartphones have created a new working culture of being constantly available and switched on – for ever checking mail, and responding after hours and on weekends. This is particularly hazardous to the type A, perfectionistic, people-pleasing personal assistant, who feels the pressure to respond in real time to anything that happens in the mailbox and feels guilty when their phone is switched off. Please look out for the section below on techno stress.

Administrative professionals may suddenly be working for more than one boss or be in a position where they are working as a team secretary, juggling tasks, managing priorities and maintaining a professional standard of work while looking after the needs of multiple stakeholders. Assistants may also be required to put on the same quality events or run the office on a much smaller budget. Our salary increases are getting smaller every year and our expenses are rising exponentially. All this creates stress that can feel overwhelming and debilitating.

The important concept to understand is that it is not necessarily the stressor, but our reaction to it that creates our stress. It is our perception that we cannot cope that creates this bad stress, not the reality of the stress itself. I hope that knowing this information will help you to see these things as challenges and not obstacles. Our point of view and our perception can assist us in these situations if we keep them positive.

Another critical factor is fatigue. When we experience stress adrenaline and other stress hormones like cortisol are being released. This makes us alert, which in turn makes it hard to switch off and get to sleep. Not being able to sleep creates fatigue, which makes you less resilient and more prone to stress, and so the vicious cycle continues. One of the most critical factors to manage when you are experiencing bad stress is your sleeping pattern. This can be done by reducing your caffeine intake, exercising more and managing your diet.

Another critical point to note is that chronic ongoing stress is much worse for you than one-off acute stress. It is the ongoing long-term exposure to stress hormones that damages neural pathways, your internal organs and causes diseased fat.

Research in the US has also found that one third of stress-related illnesses are as a direct result of bullying in the workplace, which is much more prevalent than many of us might think.

It has long been known that stress contributes to and aggravates diseases like diabetes, heart disease and hypertension. It creates blood clots, disrupts the immune system (reducing the body's healing ability by as much as 25%) and is responsible for as many as 30% of infertility cases.

Chronic and prolonged stress, and the resulting hormones released by the body, have also been proven to kill brain cells, increasing the ability of harmful chemicals and viruses to pass the blood-brain barrier.

Yes, stress is scary. But it is also a reality of the modern world that we live in. We need to be aware of its negative impact and start to manage and mitigate its harmful effects on our bodies, minds and brands. We need to arm ourselves with the theory but also implement some practical plans to reduce the impact.

Why would assistants experience stress?

Personal assistants are the frontline in the organisation (sure, this is not news!). But if you really think about it, we are surrounded by customers. Our customers are our bosses, teams and internal/external stakeholders. A few lucky assistants get to work in admin teams but the rest of us are a bit like reporters who are embedded with the army during war time (a feeling that is best understood by administrative professionals who work with engineers, architects, accountants and sales teams.) If you are lucky, you get to know them and grow close to them but your job is unique and they don't always understand (or at times value) what you do, how long things take and how difficult and thankless this job can be at times.

We also function as shock absorbers for our bosses, teams and sometimes even with external clients. Now what do I mean by that? Well, as office professionals we often take the blows meant for other people, we apologise for things that are not our fault, fix things we did not break and listen to and diffuse conflict situations not of our making.

Third, we are ultimately responsible for the quality of work that reaches the boss's desk and managing timelines of submissions. We are the final check point and we are often the one who needs to manage poor performance from direct reports (that most often outrank us).

Finally, we are expected to be on top of EVERYTHING, ALL THE TIME, NO EXCEPTIONS! The fact that we have two eyes, two ears, one brain and the same 24 hours that everyone else has is beside the point! Feeling stressed yet?

Let's face it, what makes our chosen profession so fulfilling and exciting is also what makes it very challenging at times.

Let's unpack some of the top assistant stressors:

1. Office professionals work with the top leadership of companies and have a front row seat to the action

Working in the shadow of a powerful executive can be thrilling but can also be very scary at times. You have a window into the business that few other staff on your pay grade have. You will know about instability or problems in the company and many other things that the average employee is never aware of (and doesn't have sleepless nights about). You will work the same amount of hours as your boss (in most cases) and be as connected to your smartphone as they are. Assistants who work on a senior level no longer have "working hours"; they are expected to be available 24/7.

2. Assistants have access to sensitive information and people try to access it

You have access to your boss's mail and other sources of confidential information; people know this and will at times try to exploit their relationship with you to get access to that information. It is your job to guard any information that is deemed sensitive and you may find yourself in difficult or abusive situations if you are not willing to spill the beans.

3. Assistants are expected to gate-keep and protect their bosses

We have all experienced this scenario: your boss runs into a colleague between meetings and says "sure come and see me", then gets back to the office and says that if that colleague calls or asks for a meeting you are not to schedule under any circumstances. This can be extremely stressful – you need to be professional, not damage your boss's brand but you also need to keep that individual at bay by running interference.

4. Office professionals are on the front line of technological and other changes in their offices

Assistants by virtue of their jobs need to adopt and become proficient with new office technology very quickly. Assistants often need to provide over-the-shoulder training to other team members on new software, or set up the boss's new smartphone. Technology has changed the role of the assistant over the past few decades and in my opinion will continue to do so. Change at this rate can be extremely intimidating especially if you are not technical or resistant to change.

5. Assistants need to manage the demands of the office vs. those of their homes, partners and children

Our roles are service driven and our world has become so hyper-connected we find ourselves working around the clock. Unlike the executives we support we often don't have the same assistance (driver/chauffeur, graduate/intern, cleaner, gardener, housekeeper, nanny, etc.,) or partner at home that can look after things. We need to do that too! So what happens? We work a full day in the office and then get home and do the night shift. Work-life balance and quality time with our families become neglected, creating feelings of guilt and eroding relationships.

6. Assistants need to put a smile on their face (even when they are having a bad day)

Assistants do not have the luxury of expressing the emotions that they feel or simply closing their office door (because most of us don't have one). You may be experiencing problems or heartache in your personal life but when you are in the office you need to smile, make people feel welcome and see to the needs of others. This can be incredibly draining.

7. *The assistant personality*

One of the most stressful things for assistants is often their own personalities. Most successful assistants I know are type A, perfectionists. They are driven by excellence and always strive to produce consistently superb work. This is a wonderful way to do your job but at what cost to your personal wellbeing?.

Another common problem for assistants is not being able to say "no". This places immense demands on their time and capacity to produce good work.

So why have I outlined these seven stressors above? *To depress you? To stress you?* No, rather the opposite! It is to show you that you are normal! Administrative assistants don't like others to know that they are experiencing stress or have difficulty coping. What I want you to take away from this section is that you are not alone and many other assistants are going through this too! It is not a sign of weakness on your part but rather a natural reaction to the pressures of this role. It is better for your brand to speak up than to lash out because of stress.

The good news is that we, as office professionals, are uniquely skilled to cope. We are born problem solvers and project managers. We are hugely adaptable, disciplined, resilient and capable employees. We have good relationships, which means that we can reach out and get support from others (if we ask!).

So how do you mitigate your BAD STRESS?

✓ Take a mini break. Sit outside in the sunshine, have a quick chat with a loved one or take a nice warm bath. You will feel like you can't afford the time to do this but it sometime serves as a "restart". Taking a short time-out gets you away from your problem for a time and gives you a gap to get a bit of perspective. Sometimes stepping away is the most productive thing you can do, creating a bit of space for new ideas or solutions to find you, instead of chasing them!

✓ Eat well, exercise and get enough rest. When you are feeling stress this is the last thing that you feel like doing, but these are the best coping tools at your disposal, especially exercise! Exercise uses up the excess adrenaline and stress chemicals that are swarming in and overpowering your body. If you are exercising hard you cannot maintain stressful thoughts as the focus is on physical activity, so it can give you a much needed break from the 'noise' and hectic activity taking place in your brain (a shutdown that is sometimes not even possible during sleep).

✓ Fighting fatigue and managing energy levels are the two secret weapons in the war on stress. Distress taps you out, disrupts sleep and causes you to feel lethargic. Low energy and feeling tired makes you less and less able to cope. If you cannot sleep naturally or struggle with energy levels I encourage you to seek professional help.

✓ Start planning ahead, being more organised and have a plan B. In some cases we are creating bad stress through lifestyle. Use your Sunday evening to plan, map out and mentally prepare for your week ahead. Put things away properly, have a plan in case things go wrong. Look at the small things that feed your daily stress and make plans to manage them (if you can) or accept them (if you can't).

✓ Find someone you can talk to and find activities that help you decompress. I am not advocating that you unload on people and spread misery and complaints in your wake, but rather that you find a friend (or even a professional) that you can talk to when you need to. Sometimes if we verbalise issues we get a handle on them or at least expel some of the toxic emotion associated with them.

✓ Another great tip is to take part in an activity that takes your mind off your stress completely, requires all your focus and is enjoyable (and no, that is NOT watching TV).

Lack of self-care

So what happens when we don't look after ourselves…? Unfortunately I found out the hard way. Scheduling my own doctor's appointments or taking time off to have my eyes tested or visit the dentist or when I had the flu always seemed like a luxury to me. I was working serious hours, neglecting my husband and my home and started having symptoms that I would self-medicate or simply ignore. I would skip meals and drink way too much coffee just to get through the day. Then at night I would have to take a sedative to get to sleep. The next day I would do it all over again. I felt like I worked 24 hours a day, seven days a week and could not remember what the outside of my house looked like in daylight.

So why am I telling you this? Because I know somewhere, someone is reading this right now and doing the same thing and feeling the same way…

A major incident doesn't just happen… We miss or ignore the signposts next to the road and I paid for it. Sadly so will you if you don't start managing your health and your priorities. Make sure that you take time off to rest when you need it. You are not going to get extra brownie points for being tough and you are not a machine. Taking care of yourself is not a luxury, it is an investment. You are the goose that lays the golden eggs. Don't ever forget that!

If you get to the point that you are not well enough to work you will understand what I mean by this. If you don't look after yourself it will cost you even more time off, cost you more financially, may get you into a situation where you can no longer work at all and may even ruin your relationships with your children and partner.

Luckily I am back on track but my personal experiences over the past two years have made it clear to me that we need to speak up and make sure that others in our profession start taking their own needs seriously.

Why is this a brand breaker? Well in the event that you have a medical crisis or get a divorce you will require even more time off work, you will be in bad emotional shape and it is very hard to recover a brand from this point. Prevention in this case is far better than cure. So make yourself a priority, take care of the important things and people in your life. I respect people who have a balanced outlook on their lives and know what is really important and so do most other people.

Tech stress

I have a running joke that I want the ringtone "I Believe I Can Fly" on my smartphone, because by Thursday afternoon I am ready to launch the phone at the wall. The constant beeping, ringing and pinging, the constant flood of email and calls can seriously stress me out *and I know I am not the only one.*

A study at the University of Gothenburg in Sweden on "techno stress" has found that heavy computer and cellphone use adversely affects stress levels and general mental health. The light from your computer screen disrupts your melatonin production, which disturbs your circadian cycles and damages your sleep patterns.

I often think that it would be great if we had to pay per email, then maybe people would think about their messages and ensure that they send less email of better quality. Tech stress affects anyone working in the modern world but it starts to stress your brand when you cannot manage the incoming messages and the "always-on" mode any more. You get to a point where you are so overwhelmed that you just give up. You may also lose touch with the actual people in your life – disconnecting from the reality of your life by always being connected to a device. It really is advisable to try and detox from your tech. Have a specific time in the day or at the weekend that is tech-free. This gives us some time to get away from the flood of messages but also to engage with people face to face, get out into nature, enjoy some tech-free hobbies or just be!

Have some tech rules. An example would be no smartphone to be used at the dinner table or at a restaurant with your partner – whatever will help you gain a bit of sanity and peace.

Low morale

Every single one of us (well the honest ones among us) will admit to experiencing low morale at some point during our working lives. This can be due to a multitude of reasons and circumstances. It is normal to feel low when your team has been earmarked for retrenchment; you need to arrange a champagne level function on a beer budget; or your boss has just informed you that they are leaving the company for an external position. Yes, things happen.

But we damage our brands by wallowing in these circumstances. If we don't feel like it is worth the effort anymore, others pick up on that. When you feel that your own morale is low be aware that you are most definitely having a serious ripple effect on the team as a whole. Try to regroup as soon as possible, take time off, do what you need to do to reset. But realise that this is damaging to how people perceive you and the more you entertain these feelings the more you will spiral downwards. Make plans and decisions instead!

High workload

Much like tech stress, high workload can create feelings of being completely overwhelmed and not being able to cope. When we don't feel able to cope we either give up, can't get going, start making serious mistakes or start acting out and being sarcastic and difficult to deal with.

Our roles have grown and most of us are now supporting multiple managers or teams with the same demands that we had when there were more admin staff in the organisation. And most of us are doing that for the same salary, with more hours. We are made to feel that we should be very grateful that we still have jobs at all. Sometimes it is better to admit that you are not coping with the current workload than to get to a point where you are producing poor quality work or missing deadlines. So what if people realise that you are not a superhero? If your boss/bosses don't understand or assist you once you have spoken up, at least they won't be surprised when things eventually come off the rails or you hand in a resignation letter.

We need to find smarter ways to work and as assistants we also need to learn to speak up about others' expectations. Most importantly, we must learn to ask for help when we need it.

Poor relationships and conflict in the workplace

Abusing positional power, office politics and gossiping are serious brand eroding activities that all have an adverse effect on your position in the team and the amount of respect that your peers will have for you. My advice to you would be that you manage the factors that could create conflict by being very cognisant of your own behaviour.

When conflict does occur ensure that you resolve it as amicably as possible in as short a timeframe as possible. Ongoing conflict is bad for everyone involved.

Sometimes we need to have difficult discussions, be open about what it is that is worrying us or making us upset. Sometimes talking things through can clear the air and ensure that future misunderstandings and conflict don't occur. If you don't talk things out the issues grow like cancer and one day the person involved will push your buttons for the last time causing irreparable damage.

The way you speak to others is being analysed daily. Your interactions are being observed so make sure that you do yourself proud.

Poor communication skills

Communication is an essential part of our role in our offices and in the world. We need to be able to speak well, listen carefully, be aware of our body language and write professionally.

Dr. Albert Mehrabian, who conducted various studies on non-verbal communication, found that 7% of any message is conveyed through words, 38% through certain vocal elements (tone and pace), and 55% through nonverbal elements (facial expressions, gestures, posture, etc.).

These are some powerful statistics. If only 7% is the actual content, how much quality are we losing when we rely solely on electronic messages, cutting out the body language and voice altogether? How much conflict can be avoided by picking up the phone or going to see someone face to face when dealing with a sensitive matter?

We all process the messages that we receive through our own very complex filters. The receiver of the message may misinterpret your meaning and this may cause a communication breakdown and crossed wires.

When we talk we should do so respectfully, taking into account people's differences.

As office professionals we deal with many different stakeholders so we need to be tuned into these individuals and try to communicate effectively.

When communication is misunderstood or poorly handled we can completely destroy relationships and erode our brands.

5

How you influence other people's brands and how they influence yours

You may think that your brand is only dependent on you. *Well sadly it isn't.* Many people have the ability to negatively impact or enhance our brands. We in turn have the same power and a huge responsibility. So what is the interplay between individuals and their brands?

This can manifest itself in very subtle or overt ways. People can say things about you to others, blame you or treat you with disrespect, which gives others the impression that they can do the same. My advice to you is simply this: YOU own your brand, and you are in control of your emotions. No one can make you feel inferior without your permission and those who spread lies or misrepresent you to others will be found out in the long run as long as you focus on what you need to do and do it right consistently. The wheel does turn and I have seen karma in action so do not despair.

We also need to start managing the assistants around us that give the profession a bad name –those who are really not interested in the work and are doing it because they can't find anything else to do. They go through their working days saying and doing things that reflect negatively onto us as a group. Be an example and a mentor to an individual like this or at least try and address the poor behaviour with the person, *if you can*.

The assistants I am talking about are the ones who are always saying things like "that's not my job", "this is not on my job description" or my personal favourite "I am JUST an assistant". I really dislike the last one specifically. This infers that we are somehow inferior or our jobs are low level and just operational, which they definitely are not. These assistants make it harder for the really committed ones to get the respect from business that they deserve.

Be aware that what you say and do can harm another person's brand. So always think before you speak or act. Be the person who highlights the achievements of those around you. Shine a light on those who are achieving or who are undervalued.

One of the main things that I hear from assistants (and that I am guilty of too) is that they feel that they are under-appreciated. My challenge to you is find someone else who would feel the same way and shower them with appreciation and praise. We all crave recognition for a job well done and if you are not getting it where you are then shine a light on someone else, make others feel good. The amazing thing is that you will feel good too! Start with your peers, the receptionists, security or cleaners. They make your job easier and are also not acknowledged for that either.

You and the boss

You and your boss are essentially a package deal. In my office we always joke that we are "in community of property". Your job is to make their daily life easier and more efficient and you have a direct impact on their brand (whether you realise it or not). Your boss may not even realise what a massive impact you can have directly on their personal brand but the fact is that you do!

If you don't believe me, here are three real life examples:

Scenario 1:

You call IT and very arrogantly insist that someone come to your office immediately to assist with an issue. You make sure they <u>KNOW</u> that you work for someone very important and you are not willing to wait even five minutes for a support person to arrive.

Sure, you got the performance, but at what cost? The technician who came out may be on a junior level and never meet your manager face to face, but what impression have you created of yourself and your boss? Is it one of arrogance and entitlement? Do you really think that individual won't go back to their office and tell others about your behaviour? Do you really think that word won't get around the company in time if you behave like this consistently? And when the story is retold, they will say "the CFO's office" or the CFO, not the assistant at the CFO's office.

Scenarios 2 and 3 come from my own personal experiences (I just HAD to share).

Scenario 2:

I started working for a lady a few years ago and everyone told me how aloof and stand-offish she was. How she thought she was better than everyone else and was very high maintenance. A few months later the same people who had made these remarks to me realised that it was in fact the previous assistant that had been telling them this and it was her behaviour (and not the boss's) that had created that impression…. Scary but true.

Our bosses spend a great deal of time in meetings and behind closed doors. We are their ambassadors and we can seriously tarnish their brands if we are not careful.

Scenario 3:

The other story is about a gentleman I worked for. He was ALWAYS late. It didn't matter who he was meeting with and this behaviour was ongoing. He would often blame me if he arrived late, saying things like I added the wrong directions to his calendar or double booked him (which was not true). So of course what happens in a case like this is that people think you are incompetent and cannot do your job. On the upside, when this behaviour is ongoing – and as they get to know the other person – they start seeing through this behaviour and they ultimately know who is to blame.

I am sure that some of you will relate to the two stories above and may even have experienced something similar. I have retold them here so that you can see some examples of how our brands overlap and how we are enhancing or eroding each other's brands by our behaviour and what we are telling others.

Always be aware that you are responsible for the impression you make and for the image you project of your office, manager and company. So if you behave badly or act inappropriately it impacts others too. Be considerate always!

You and your colleagues

We have all had that one colleague who will let you down consistently just to make you look bad in the eyes of the boss. They will go out of their way to sabotage you when you work together making sure that you are left holding the bag by either not helping you with information you need or by submitting their part of the project to you at the very last minute putting you under pressure to get the job done in time. They are actively trying to destroy your credibility and damage your brand. They do this for various reasons but often it is because of their own insecurity, jealousy or jockeying for position within your team.

These kinds of actions can have a terrible impact on your brand. In this situation it is very important to document your actions and keep your manager in the loop so that when something goes wrong you have the proof that you did what you could.

Colleagues may also spread gossip about you or misrepresent what you have said to others thereby tarnishing your brand. There is not much that one can do about this kind of behaviour. My biggest piece of advice to you is to do the right things right and let karma take care of the rest. If you are consistent and authentic the other person will be found out (usually by their own bad behaviour).

I also want to encourage you to refrain from making yourself guilty of this kind of behaviour. Often you have a very close relationship with your manager and they put real value in your opinions and observations. Don't abuse this position to sabotage or hurt the careers of your colleagues out of pettiness. This is not good for your continued position of trust or for your brand long term.

Be cognisant of the fact that what you say and do has repercussions. If something you have heard via the grapevine is unconfirmed, treat it as such. Don't get sucked into office politics and gossip. It is one of the ugliest and most destructive activities that you can participate in. It is negative and if you engage in it you are actively helping to perpetuate this as a culture within your organisation.

You and your family and friends

Many of you read the title of this section and thought "how on earth can my friends or family damage my brand at work?" Well it's actually very simple.

Do you have a friend at work who spends way too much time at your desk chatting and you can't find a polite way to get them to leave? *What is your boss quietly thinking?* Could they be thinking that you don't take the work that you need to do seriously? That you are lazy and/or a bit too social? Your manager may even worry that you are talking about sensitive work related matters with this person (even if you are not).

In the case of family you may have a partner that interferes with your work life in an inappropriate way, getting involved with your boss or colleagues when they are not happy with how you were treated. Or you may have a child that is often ill causing you to be away from work more than you would like. These are just some simple examples of how family and friends can create a bad impression of you.

Now, if your family member or friend really cares about you they will understand that you need to change certain behaviours to save face. An honest and open discussion may be uncomfortable but necessary. Look at your own circumstances and find the people who are affecting your brand who may not be based in your office or company. See what you can change and do it!

You and your stakeholders – vendors/clients

Perhaps you are working on a customer complaint. You are doing everything you can to help the customer but they just don't like you and feel that progress is not as fast as it could be (yet you are doing absolutely everything in your power). This person gets into direct contact with your boss and complains. How does this make you look?

Or you delay in responding to a meeting request and the customer runs into your manager/s at an event and indicates they have been waiting for you to respond.

Neither one of these scenarios makes you look good. There are many more examples of how the interaction between you and customers can impact your brand and I think if you look at your working day you could find many more. It is important that you manage their expectations, and be transparent and professional when you interact with external parties.

Vendors are another story altogether. How often has a supplier made a commitment to you and not lived up to their end of the bargain? It has happened to me many times in my career. It has a way of making you look like you are incompetent or that you can't plan properly. Following up with vendors, ensuring that they understand what you need and managing their performance is absolutely critical in safeguarding your brand in the long run.

6

Brand recovery strategy

Brand Recovery Activity Worksheet

30-day plan with an activity to try per day/focus area

It's time to get stuck in, and do some practical work on your brand. I hope you are excited about the process and that you will approach these activities with an open mind and heart.

At this point I would recommend that you get either a notebook or start an electronic document for the notes and observations that you will be making for the next month. These notes will be important not only to crystallise your thoughts. Personally I find that once we put pen to paper (or fingers to keyboard) we have a clearer, more defined plan and a better handle on the matters before us. I encourage you to really take your time with each exercise.

Use as much or as little time as you need for each day's focus area (*in fact if you need more than a day to finish the activity, then do exactly that*). This is your time to work on

YOU. Invest in this seriously and I assure you that your results will improve.

Try to consistently apply the activities or tasks; the aim is to use your imagination and your creativity to bring these activities into your world. This should not be an academic exercise but an exploration. And if you miss a day, no problem, just start again as soon as you are able to. Naturally your level of commitment and focus will determine your personal results. I hope you are ready, let's begin!

Day 1: Complete the Brand Health Assessment

If you have not yet done so, now is the perfect time to take the brand health assessment earlier in this book. You can also complete it online at http://www.anelmartin.co.za/brand-health-assessment.html. This will give you some insight into what needs your attention.

Which habits, activities, behaviours and relationships need to be worked on? To achieve success, some serious introspection will be required during the next 30 days. If you have already completed the questionnaire now is the time to review it in detail. If you are really serious about your own brand recovery/revamp/improvement you will need to commit and give this your full attention and set aside some time in your schedule for the foreseeable future. The more disciplined you are during this period, the more long term benefits you can expect and the faster your improvements will manifest themselves.

The focus areas for each level of brand health are as follows:

- Excellent health: your goal is improvement and refinement. The aim for you is to position yourself as a premium and desirable brand.

- Average health: your goal is to elevate your performance. The step up from good to great. Special attention should be given to your unique features and daily routines

- Poor health: your goal is to really get back to basics, identify the spheres that you are letting yourself down in and formulate a plan that you can put into action to create a full brand turnaround.

Your baseline at this point is irrelevant, what matters is that you have decided to take on the challenge and you are ready to take your performance up a level.

Day 2: What does MY ideal brand look like?

Today I would like you to explore what your perfect brand looks like. Again a tip of the hat to author Steven Covey in *7 Habits of Highly Effective People*: "We are going to begin with the end in mind". How will you know that you have achieved the brand that you really want? Well it's simple! You need to know what it will look and feel like. In today's activity I want you to take your time defining what this means to you.

- Here are some questions to get you going:

- How would you like your manager and team to see you?

- What do you want others to say about you professionally *and perhaps even personally?*

- What are the competencies, habits and behaviours that you would like to be known and respected for?

- What is the value/legacy that you want to add to your world?

Are you a little stuck? Think about the assistants you respect. What is it about them that you admire? Maybe you don't know another inspirational assistant (that would be really sad), then look at the world around you. Perhaps your role model is your mother, someone in your company, a respected global entrepreneur; maybe it's a combination of traits from many different people. It makes no difference where your inspiration comes from, but take some time to really think about your perfect brand scenario. Make it as detailed and as vivid as you can. Remember that truly successful brands don't only look good, *they are good!* They are authentic, they offer value and they are desirable.

I really want you to make your notes come alive – stick pictures, create a vision board, a presentation/video or audio reminder, use different colour pens. In fact, use **ANYTHING** which makes this experience interactive and meaningful to you. The work you do today will serve as a constant reminder to you of what you want to achieve and as such it should be INSPIRATIONAL and easily accessible to you. The end product should motivate and excite you!

Why is this process so important? Well, it's simple. If we don't know where we are going, then how on earth will we know when we get there? How will we know if we are lost or have taken a serious detour? You are establishing the requirements of your revamp and in doing this activity thoughtfully, it will show you what you need to work on, what you really value and what you are already really fantastic at! Enjoy this activity and remember this is for you and about you. Be a bit selfish and spend some time on setting the scene and mapping your journey ahead.

Day 3: Today vs the future

Yesterday we played, dreamed and visualised. Today I want us to come back to the reality at hand. We need to be very honest. It's time to look in the mirror, without judgement. Nobody is perfect and we ALL still have room for improvement. Today we need to analyse and unpack the development and improvement areas. Below I have given you a few prompts to get you started:

- How far apart are your ideal and your current brand? [%]

- What are the obvious things that come to mind that need work?

- What negative feedback do you consistently get about your performance?

- In which spheres of your work do you feel that you are working below your level of ability?

- What could you easily improve with a bit more effort?

- What emotions or bad habits are holding you back from having your ideal brand?

Wow, this is some heavy stuff…

The idea here is not to make you negative or get you to beat yourself up. By exploring the gaps we are formulating a custom action plan of what we want to work on. What is at the top of your mind? What activities will produce the most visible and valuable results? What small tweaks will get you big outcomes? Which relationships need work? What are you neglecting?

Day 4: Top five development goals

Yesterday may not have been a fun activity to complete but you did it. Give yourself a big round of applause! You gave the gaps you have identified some serious thought and today we are going to get practical and make plans. I need you to list your top five areas of improvement.

Once you have done that, I want you to write down some ways that you can work on and mitigate these issues:

- What training do you require?

- What behaviour changes do you need to make?

- Who do you know who can assist you with these problem areas?

- Is there anyone who can function as a mentor or coach to you?

- Are there company training programmes or other formal avenues that you can follow to get support?

- Are you ready to take charge and make changes?

- Can you drop the excuses and the victim mentality?

The questions above are just to get the ball rolling. The idea is that you find solutions. They need to be practical. Remember that these action items do not need to be massive or time consuming. Focus on what you can do in small increments to chip away at the problem areas. Be cognisant of the time constraints you face in your working life and be pragmatic in this regard. Only take on what you can commit to and what you know you can achieve, otherwise you will only make yourself feel worse for not achieving what you set out to do. Rome wasn't built in a day and neither is a great brand – so take it day by day in baby steps.

Once you have made plans you need to plot them on a timeline. I would recommend assigning a development area (one of your five) to each day of the working week. Set aside 30mins each day, make it part of your new routine until these areas are managed.

Example:

Monday – emotional intelligence and relationship building

Activity:

- Instead of emailing try to make more calls today

- Try to meet one new person or chat to someone I don't know in the elevator

- Sincerely thank or compliment a colleague

- Greet everyone that works close to me when I come in and leave for the day

- Think about how my behaviour affects others

Tuesday – Microsoft Office skills touch up

Activity:

- Learn one new keyboard shortcut

- Learn one new functionality in Excel/Word/PowerPoint/other

Wednesday – attention to detail

Activity: XXX

You get the picture.

Add these items as a daily meeting to your diary or online calendar (call it your T5 Time) and try to be disciplined about doing what you commit to. Keeping promises to yourself makes you feel good and gives you confidence. Try to make this a routine. Some days the craziness of the office will not allow you to get to your T5. Don't play catch up, just move on to the next day's tasks. Some days this will feel like a luxury that you can't afford but what you really need to consider is what happens to you and your employability if you don't start working on your problem areas. The choice is yours!

Hopefully in time you will chip away at these problem areas and then you can change your T5 and start working on new items. I absolutely adore motivational speaker and life coach Tony Robbins and he says, "Your rituals will determine your results." By making these small daily activities part of your routine I know that you will see a quantum leap of improvement over time. Good Luck!

Day 5: So what's special about ME?

I can almost guarantee that today's activity will be harder for you to complete than yesterday's was. It's human nature to focus on your weaknesses and what you think you are not good at (sometimes completely made up and in your own mind). Sadly, when I do this part in workshops people often draw a blank. It's not that they don't have any special abilities or talents, they have just never thought about it, explored or verbalised it.

It is really hard to speak up in front of others and say "I am really good at X" or "Y is an exceptional ability of mine", but remember that as a brand you will need to "sell" yourself. Part of the reason that others will "buy" into you and your brand are the things that make you unique and special. This could be the difference between getting the job and not getting it.

So what do we need to do specifically today?

- List at LEAST three super powers (special skills)

- If you cannot list them yourself consult with a colleague, your manager or partner

- **DO NOT MOVE ON FROM THIS ACTIVITY UNTIL YOU HAVE THREE**

Like your development areas these will now become diarised on a quarterly basis.

Example:

JAN/FEB/MAR/APR – Communication Skills

MAY/JUN/JUL/AUG – Organisational skills and logistics

SEPT/OCT/NOV/DEC – Creativity

During these four-month cycles I want you to find activities, training and opportunities to use and enhance these skills.

Talk to your manager to assign you to a project where you can use your "super power", get additional formal training to enhance this skill, read a book about enhancing this skill or find someone you can teach your special skill to.

The most important part of this exercise is finding your "super power" so make this a priority. Once identified, it will be easy and fun to put it to good use. This will not only benefit you but also your team, manager and company. Good careers are built on your strengths, so embrace what you are good at and use it to add value in your world. You will find this exhilarating and fulfilling because you will be good at it. This will increase your confidence in leaps and bounds and will get you noticed for the right reasons.

Day 6: My daily routine in focus

For today, simply track your routine:

- What time do I get up?

- What do I do before work?

- What do I do first thing as I get to work?

- How much time do I spend on email?

- How much time do I spend on other activities and what are they?

- How much time do I spend on non-work-related activities and interactions?

- How many interruptions did I have today?

- What time do I leave work?

- What is my evening routine?

- Was I anxious or relaxed?

- Did I feel rushed?

- Was I on the back foot or feeling like I was ahead of the curve?

Day 7: My daily routine in focus – did I like what I saw?

Yesterday we simply observed a normal working day. Today we need to decide if we liked what we saw.

- Were you late for work?

- Did you get stuck in traffic that you could have avoided?

- Did you waste time drinking coffee with friends or chatting in the kitchen?

- Where you on social media or personal calls for a long period of time?

- What was your evening routine like with your family? Do you feel you neglected them?

- Did you rush around from dawn till dusk?

- How were your interactions with those around you?

- Where you really productive or just busy?

- Were you in a constant state of anxiety or worry?

- Did you add any value to the people around you?

- Did you do ANYTHING today that your future self will thank you for?

Remember that if we do what we have always done, we will get what we have always got. It's time to break the chain. For many of us the working week can be like the movie *Groundhog Day* where we experience the same day over and over again. The alarm goes off at the same time, you make a cup of coffee, pour a bath, get dressed, get to the office, start the day, put out the required amount of fires, leave the office late, rush home, have to make dinner or help the kids with their homework, do more work, tidy up, get to bed... *And the next day we do it all over again!*

In our focus on serving others we neglect the activities that move us forward. If we don't do anything today that will make things better tomorrow, we should hardly be surprised if we don't move forward in life, if we don't reach our goals or make progression in life. It's a hard reality to face for a busy assistant I know.

What did you like about your day? What didn't you like about your day? What would you really like to change that is going to make all the difference in the long run? Write it down!

Days 8 – 12: Five days of "small things"

There are always small changes that we can make that will change how effective we are. For the next five days we will be focusing on the quick wins. The activities I want you to zoom in on are the tiny things that snowball or create a ripple effect. These are the routine activities that we tend to neglect that can seriously trip us up on the most unexpected and inconvenient day.

Activities like:

- Creating a to-do list and keeping it up to date

- Getting your mailbox down to a manageable level

- Sorting out your desk and your filing

- Making sure that you double check all the items on the calendar the day before to ensure that there are no nasty surprises

- Checking that you have stationery in stock

- Setting up regular face-to-face meetings with your boss or setting up a regular call

- Creating a system for documents coming in and going out of your office

- Updating your mailing lists or contacts

These are just some of the examples of the "small things" you can do, which are relatively routine, and which can make your life easier in the long run, but can be neglected when you are fighting fires all the time. Yes, and again I hear you saying, "But Anel, I hardly have time to get through my normal work in the day, where on earth will I find time for these nice-to-have items?"

Well in response to that I just want to ask you:

- How bad does it feel when you forget to do something the boss asked you to do?

- How unprofessional do you look when you are not aware of or miss an important email because your mailbox is too full?

- How much time have you wasted in the last month looking for stuff in your drawers or on your desk because it is untidy?

And so on and on… I think you get my point. Now you need to MAKE TIME to SAVE TIME!

Day 12: What are your observations after your week of "small things"?

Today just reflect on your week of "small things". Did it make you feel good? Did it feel like a waste of time? Do you feel more organised and in control? There are no right or wrong answers. If you found this helpful do you think there are more "small things" you should target? Did anyone notice you working on the "small things"? Do you think that "small things" should get a bit of time each week going forwards?

Day 13: Procrastinating – the enemy of energy

We all have tasks that we dread doing, items that remain on our to-do lists much longer than they should. Putting items off takes more mental energy than just getting them done, makes you feel guilty and like a bit of a loser. Procrastinating is never good for your brand, especially if you want others to see you as reliable, efficient and competent. Procrastinating or making excuses (even to yourself) about things that you should get done erodes your self-worth and confidence.

- What tasks do you genuinely dislike?

- Is there a reason you don't like the task? Do you not understand what you need to do? Is it boring? Do you feel someone else is responsible for it and it was dumped on you? Try to identify the root cause of your dislike

- Now that you have actually thought about why you don't like it, does it make it any easier to complete the task? Can you change the way you feel about it or perceive it? Is there someone who can show you how to do it?

- Can you put all these kinds of activities into one block of time and just push through it to get it done and dusted?

- What time of day are you mentally at your best? When during the day do you have the most patience? What time are you most alert and ready to do something challenging?

- Which day of the week would you say you feel the most focused, confident and able to get things done?

Today, I want you to look at your list of items that you consistently put off. Try to establish the ideal time of day and perhaps even time of the week to tackle them. Try to get these matters closed off. It is much more draining thinking about these things than tackling them. Tie up your loose ends! You will feel so relieved and accomplished when they are done and I encourage you to tackle these items on an ongoing basis. Doing things we don't enjoy takes discipline but the good news is that the more we practise being disciplined the easier it will become. Being a successful assistant (or person in general) often means that you are willing to do the things others are not willing to do. Claim back your control over yourself and your energy by procrastinating less.

Day 14: Relationships

Today I want you to identify two relationships (one personal and one professional) that really need your attention.

- Who have you been neglecting because of your schedule?

- Who is that one person you cannot see eye to eye with?

- Which relationship creates negative feelings in your life?

- Is communication breaking down?

- Are you too sensitive or is the other party?

- Are you holding a grudge?

- Can this relationship be salvaged and changed?

- Is it time to move on or can this relationship improve?

- What can YOU do to improve the situation?

- Are you always focusing on the other person's bad qualities and behaviours?

- Can you release your desire for the other person to change first?

- Who do you need to thank or apologise to?

- Who needs the gift of your time?

Relationships are an essential part of our lives and negative relationships have a deep and lasting impact on us and on how others perceive us. We need to decide what is worth working on, what we need to let go of and when we simply need to agree to disagree and treat the person with more respect than they give us. Taking the high road is always the recommended route. It is much, much harder but it will be worth it in the end for your emotional health and for your brand.

I encourage you, as far as possible (and as far as is healthy) to try and rebuild these damaged relationships, not for the benefit of the other party but for your own. You cannot have peace when you are in conflict or even anticipate conflict. If you have reached the end of the road with the other person make a decision to move beyond this relationship (even if this means finding another job).

It is important for you to list concrete actions for each of these relationships. What are you going to **do**? What do you take responsibility for? What can you change? What must you accept? What must you end?

Day 15: The halfway mark

Today we reach the halfway mark. So, fifteen days in, what's going on with you?

- Are you feeling any different about yourself, your working day, your relationships and your brand?

- Has anything interesting happened since you started on this challenge?

- Are you noticing anything changing within yourself?

- Are you looking at things a little differently?

- Are you still on track?

- Do you feel that the last few days have added value to you?

- Are you sticking to your T5 activities?

- What have you learnt?

I simply want you to reflect today and try to gauge what has happened to you and around you over the past few days. I hope that you are feeling focused and that you are making significant gains.

Day 16: Social media review

Today I want you to log on to your various social media accounts. Honestly access the content and photos that you post. Review this as a neutral observer or imagine that you are an HR manager recruiting for a prestigious assistant position with an incredible company. What are your impressions?

- How do your profile photos look?

- Anything on your timeline that makes you cringe?

- Are there lots of posts about how sick you are? Or how much you hate your job? Or how much Monday sucks? Or how much you drank last weekend?

- Any posts that can be considered controversial or offensive?

- Any photos or posts that you would rather not have had our imaginary HR recruiter see?

- Do you not have an online presence at all?

What's on the internet can never be deleted or undone. But going forward, commit to yourself that you will manage your social media responsibly. Make sure that your LinkedIn profile is current (not something you set up three years ago which is completely outdated) and that it has a photograph and that all your other profiles are the best possible reflection of you.

For those of you who are not active on social media, I strongly encourage you to sign up today. You are missing out on an opportunity to increase your network and influence. There are various exceptional assistant resources on social media today and I would encourage you to join such forums on Facebook, Twitter and LinkedIn. I personally guarantee it will add great value to your career.

If you are new to social media or a bit fearful then make a deal with one of your colleagues who may be better at it and trade assistance. Let them guide you on social media and teach them something that you are good at. This can a fun, bonding experience and is beneficial to both parties!

Days 17 and 18: CV days

Today and tomorrow we are talking about your CV. When was yours last updated?

I would like you to set aside some time to bring this document (catalogue of your services) up to date. As mentioned earlier in this book, a CV is a living document and you should always have it on standby. You never know when your circumstances may change or an incredible opportunity present itself.

Things to review and update:

- Is the format I am using a good one?

- Check formatting and spelling

- Check the actual information. Is it accurate? Is it fully up to date?

- Am I positioning myself properly or is this document filled with clichés?

- Do I need someone to assist me with this?

- What would make my CV stand out from the crowd?

Day 19: Taking control of stress

Yes, I know, I constantly come back to stress but it really is very important in the context of this subject. Managing stress alleviates so many of the brand breakers automatically. Being aware of how you function when you are stressed makes so many things clear. So today we look at what stresses you out. Make a list of your top-five stressors (work or personal). Do they cause bad stress, good stress or acute stress?

Day 20: Stress busting

Now that we know what your triggers are for stress, what can you actually do about them?

- Can you influence the event or thing that is creating your stress?

- Can you get someone to help you?

- Do you need to learn how to relax and release the stress?

- Do you create stress for yourself if there is nothing to stress about?

- What concrete action can you take to mitigate your stress?

- If you cannot change your stress, can you at least learn to accept your circumstances and deal with your stress in a healthier way?

Look at your list of five top stressors. Define an action or a decision for each and try to implement it for the next week.

Days 21-25: Stress-busting implementation week

For the next five days I want you to start implementing your actions or decisions regarding your top five stressors. This should be an ongoing action item not limited to the next five days – but try to really focus on it this week. Put your plans into action and try to get some traction on this matter.

Day 26: Stress management outcomes

So, for the last week you have been trying to manage your stress. Maybe you left earlier for work to avoid the stress of sitting in traffic and being late every morning. Perhaps you had a difficult discussion with your manager that you should have had a long time ago. It could be that you set aside two hours on a Saturday to get to grips with your overflowing mailbox.

Whatever you did this week, congrats! As soon as you focus on what you do have control over, you suddenly feel more able to cope and you see results.

- What was the best outcome of the week?

- What did you learn?

- Did nothing change?

- Is stress part of your personality or something that is happening externally?

Day 27: Take a day to play!

What do you really enjoy? What recharges your batteries? Is it reading to your children, having a nice hot bath or walking the dogs? Today I want you to reward yourself. Do something you enjoy, it doesn't have to take a lot of time or cost money. Going forwards, I want you to think about the small things in life that give you joy, and make time for these on a regular basis.

Find a hobby, read a book for relaxation, take your friend for a coffee or book a full day in the spa for yourself, whatever that thing is for you. Sometimes we are so busy working and serving the needs of others that we forget to LIVE. We forget to feed our souls and that we need time to recharge. My challenge to you is reward yourself with a little pleasure today and more regularly going forward.

Day 28: Let's prepare for a your performance appraisal discussion

Hopefully you have a job description and well-defined key performance indicators. It's time to review these documents (or create them if you don't already have them).

Your job description and key performance indicators (KPIs) define what you are actually supposed to be doing during a working day. But I have always felt that performance appraisals for assistants are very subjective indeed. It all hinges on your relationship with your manager/s and how they rate your service to them.

- Take your KPIs and do a self-assessment

- Look at your self-assessment. Are you happy with your performance?

- What actions can you take to improve the current performance?

- What competencies need work?

- How do you address the gaps when it comes to your competencies?

- What training and support do you need to up your game?

- What activities are really taking up time and are not listed on your job description or KPI document?

- How can you reduce these activities or do they need to be added?

- What have you done in the past year which was above and beyond what is listed on your KPIs? Any special projects?

Take some time to really understand what you are meant to be doing and how your manager/s will rate your performance. If anything is unclear schedule a meeting and get the clarification that you need as soon as you can.

Going forwards, track all the extras that you do so that you can add them to your portfolio of evidence at performance appraisal time.

Sadly, no matter how good you are at your job you may not get a fair performance appraisal when the time comes. But always know that if you work hard and show commitment other opportunities will present themselves. This is the cornerstone of your brand in the working world.

Day 29: Get feedback – is anyone else seeing the difference?

Yes, we are almost done. I hope the past few days have helped you and put things into perspective for you.

It's time to reach out and get feedback.

Did anyone notice that you were working on your brand? Has your boss made comments about your new approach? It's time to engage with those who are close to you and get some input.

Day 30: REVIEW YOUR PROGRESS TO DATE AND SCHEDULE YOUR NEXT BRAND ASSESSMENT

Today is our very last day of the Brand Building Challenge. I want you to look back on the past 30 days:

- Did anything change?

- How are you feeling?

- What did you learn?

- What will you continue doing?

And, finally, I would recommend that you keep working hard and re-take the Brand Health Assessment at regular intervals to see if you have improved and how you are progressing.

Well done! I am thrilled with your hard work and dedication during this challenge. You have the ground work in place. I wish you well for the continued success of your brand and your career!

7

Conclusion

A successful brand is really the sum of its parts. It is not one particular element and it is not created using a single recipe. Your brand will be completely unique because you truly are a one-off edition.

In closing it is my sincere hope that this book has given you the quality time to look at yourself objectively and the tools to start constructing a brand intentionally and with purpose, not merely living with the results of what has happened to date. You are the engineer. You now have the plan, the building is entirely up to you.

I hope it has helped you gain some self-knowledge and that you can now better identify people whose behaviour you can respect and emulate. I also hope it has helped you become aware of your own brand and those of the people around you. And that long term you will reap the rewards of doing the work.

The goal for me was to share some of my own personal light-bulb moments in the hope that it would give you some things to think about and perhaps a few things to try and work on. Thank you for taking this journey with me and please reach out to me to share your success stories or get additional advice.

Acknowledgements

I would be completely remiss if I did not thank and acknowledge some individuals who have been influential in my professional life. First, Lucy Brazier, who gave me my very first opportunity to put my thoughts to paper and share them with a wider audience – she has been a mentor and a guiding light. Victoria Darragh, who saw my article, "Building a Powerful PA Brand", which led to my first invitation to present internationally at the 2013 Hays PA event. This set the wheels in motion to change the trajectory of my career. My ladies, Susan Engelbrecht, Marti Beukes, Cathy Harris, Michele Thwaits and Teri Wells, who have been the most incredible role models and teachers. They have taught me with every interaction (very often without even realising it). They have shown me what the top-tier assistants do and say. They have always believed in me and I am so grateful for their support. This book and many other things would not have been possible without their influence and involvement. Finally, I want to thank each and every delegate and assistant that I have had the chance to meet over the past few years. You have been an inspiration and a fountain of new ideas. I am in awe of the assistants working in the world today and I want to acknowledge how incredible and special each and every single one of you are! Live your truth and SHINE!

38498797R00067

Printed in Poland
by Amazon Fulfillment
Poland Sp. z o.o., Wrocław